W9-BWR-383

Dreaming

Dreaming

An Opportunity for Change

Myron L. Glucksman

JASON ARONSON
Lanham • Boulder • New York • Toronto • Plymouth, UK

Published in the United States of America
by Jason Aronson
An imprint of Rowman & Littlefield Publishers, Inc.

A wholly owned subsidiary of
The Rowman & Littlefield Publishing Group, Inc.
4501 Forbes Boulevard, Suite 200, Lanham, Maryland 20706
www.rowmanlittlefield.com

Estover Road
Plymouth PL6 7PY
United Kingdom

British Library Cataloguing in Publication Information Available

Library of Congress Cataloging-in-Publication Data

Glucksman, Myron L.
 Dreaming : an opportunity for change / Myron L. Glucksman.
   p. ; cm.
 Includes bibliographical references.
 ISBN-13: 978-0-7657-0447-4 (cloth : alk. paper)
 ISBN-10: 0-7657-0447-1 (cloth : alk. paper)
 ISBN-13: 978-0-7657-0448-1 (pbk. : alk. paper)
 ISBN-10: 0-7657-0448-X (pbk. : alk. paper)
 1. Dreams. 2. Dream interpretation. 3. Psychoanalysis. I. Title.
 [DNLM: 1. Dreams—psychology. 2. Psychoanalytic Therapy. 3. Psychoanalytic
Interpretation. WM 460.5.D8 G567d 2006]
 BF175.5.D74G58 2007
 154.6'3—dc22   2006017492

Printed in the United States of America

♾^{TM} The paper used in this publication meets the minimum requirements of American
National Standard for Information Sciences—Permanence of Paper for Printed Library
Materials, ANSI/NISO Z39.48-1992.

Contents

Contents

Preface

The concept for this book evolved over many years of clinical practice and teaching. When I was in psychoanalytic training, the "classical," or Freudian, theory of dreaming heavily influenced my understanding of the function of dreams. That is, dreams were considered to be initiated by sexual or aggressive impulses that required censorship in order to preserve sleep. Subsequent sleep and dream research, as well as continued modification of the psychoanalytic theories of dreaming, helped me to appreciate the biological substrate of dreaming and its adaptive functions. Rather than viewing the dream exclusively as a censorship mechanism of instinctual drives, I have come to understand it as a biologically based, metaphorical presentation of the dreamer's wishes, conflicts, feelings, relationships, problems, and self-identity.

Earlier in my career, the process of free association and dream interpretation seemed a mysterious and intuitive enterprise. However, my training analyst, Irving Bieber, always searched for the major theme in a dream, and that made a lasting impression on me. One of my psychoanalytic mentors, Walter Bonime, particularly emphasized feelings and relationships in dream content. He was a master at connecting associative material to the patient's deepest emotions and interpersonal pathology. His book, *The Clinical Use of Dreams*, remains one of the most informative texts illustrating the collaborative interaction between therapist and client in working with dreams. In my own clinical practice, I gradually developed an approach toward understanding dreams using what I learned from supervisors, colleagues, and patients. As a supervisor of psychiatric residents and psychoanalytic candidates, I taught my method of free association and dream interpretation in order to help them make sense out of their patients' dreams. For me, free association is more meaningful when it consists of a dialogue between client and therapist, rather than an uninterrupted stream of consciousness on the part of the client. I believe that the therapist requires some type of road map in order to obtain relevant information during the free association process. In order to accomplish this, I keep in mind various arbitrary categories of free association connected to the dream manifest content. These consist of themes, feelings, surroundings, activities, people, and self-portrayals. Collectively, these components can serve as a guide for both therapist and client to translate the associative material into the essential meaning of the dream.

   Throughout my career, especially in my clinical research, I have had an interest in the factors that promote clinical change during psychotherapy. Operationally, I divide clinical change into two basic categories: (1) intrapsychic, or internal, and (2) behavioral, or external. Intrapsychic, or internal, change includes affective regulation, defensive reorganization, modification of internal objects and self-representations, conflict or problem resolution, cognitive restructuring, and internal awareness. Behavioral, or external, change includes actions, implementation of decisions, communication, interpersonal behavior, and adaptability. As I worked with my patients, it became apparent to me that their dreams during treatment reflected various aspects of internal and external change. For example, while the dreams of a clinically depressed patient frequently contained themes of hopelessness and social withdrawal during the early phase of treatment, they increasingly reflected themes of optimism and interaction with others during the later phase of treatment. Likewise, while the dreams of a patient in an abusive marital relationship contained recurrent themes of dependency and victimization during the early phase of therapy, they more frequently contained themes of independence and increased self-esteem during the later phase of therapy. I concluded that these changes in dream content provided a useful validation of what my patients and I observed and experienced at a conscious level during treatment. In turn, this led me to think about the relationship between dreams and the various clinical elements involved in the psychotherapeutic process. As a result, I arbitrarily differentiate dreams according to the major issues or topics addressed in the manifest and latent content. These include feelings, relationships, self-identity, problem solving and decision making, wish-fulfillment, life crisis, trauma, and termination. Within these categories are dreams primarily concerned with transference, countertransference, resistance, and salient conflicts. Most dreams, of course, contain several or all of these elements, and my classification is primarily for educational and research purposes. The major point to be made is that many dreams are intimately connected with the psychotherapeutic process and contain one or more elements associated with clinical change. Recently, my colleague Milton Kramer and I examined the relationship between dream manifest content and clinical change during treatment. Our observations suggested that the manifest content of selected dreams during psychotherapy correlates significantly with the clinical course of the client. Therefore, we concluded that dreams can be used as a reliable index of progress or lack thereof during treatment. This finding has important implications for the assessment of outcome in psychotherapy.

Dreams not only validate change throughout the course of treatment, but they can also facilitate change when they are understood and applied by the dreamer. Like poems or paintings, their metaphorical imagery is often powerful and incisive. The adage "one picture is worth a thousand words" applies equally to dream imagery. More than a century after Sigmund Freud proclaimed the dream to be the "royal road" to the unconscious, it remains our most important avenue toward understanding mentation outside of conscious awareness. In my opinion, dreams provide a continuous, symbolic commentary on our internal psychological (and sometimes physical) functions. Whenever language fails to convey a particular inner experience, dream imagery can capture it vividly and authentically. The entire spectrum of human emotions, conflicts, interactions, and perceptions can be presented by dream content pointedly and dramatically. The dreamer can use this imagery to achieve greater insight, as well as improvement in self-functioning and relationships with others. During psychotherapy, dreams can often facilitate the client's awareness of central conflicts, feelings, relationships, and self-identity with greater clarity than can be achieved consciously. The ideal goal of working with a dream during psychotherapy is for the client and therapist to arrive at a mutually agreed upon interpretation or understanding of the dream imagery. Interpretation does not necessarily mean a singular view of the dream. There may be one or more interpretations that provide complimentary or even conflicting viewpoints on the dream. However, of far greater importance than interpretations are the various perspectives, connections, and emotions that free association elicits. In turn, the client can utilize this information to bring about both internal and external change. Certain dreams, including problem-solving, decision-making, and turning-point dreams, are particularly effective in facilitating change. At the very least, the increased self-awareness that results from working with dream material constitutes a form of change. Individuals who have learned to work with dreams during psychotherapy can continue to monitor and understand their dreams following treatment. This gives them the opportunity to engage in an ongoing process of internal and external change.

My initial goal in writing this book was to provide therapists and dreamers with a methodology for understanding dream imagery and to use that knowledge for the purpose of change. Because of the unique position dreams hold in the psychotherapeutic process, I felt it was necessary to integrate dreaming with various clinical aspects of psychotherapy. As a result, I have paid particular attention to such issues as conflict and problem resolution, psychodynamics, transference, countertransference, resistance, trauma, and termination. Nevertheless, I have tried to keep the book focused on a method of understanding dreams for the purpose of personal growth and change, both within and outside of the context of therapy. Although it is written primarily for mental-health professionals, I believe that nonprofessionals with experience in psychotherapy and an interest in dreams can also benefit from it. Because of my medical background, I am conditioned to use the term *patient* instead of *client*. I consider these terms interchangeable, although in this book I use the term *client* for those individuals who are in psychotherapy.

Finally, I owe a debt of gratitude to those who helped and inspired me to engage in this project. They include the numerous individuals I have treated over the years who have shared and worked on their dreams with me. The changes that occurred in their personalities and lives motivated me to write this book. For purposes of confidentiality, their identities and histories have been disguised in the dream illustrations I have provided. In addition, I am extremely grateful to my many teachers, colleagues, and students who stimulated my thinking and contributed to my knowledge on this topic. In particular, I wish to thank my friend and colleague Roman Anshin for his continued encouragement and valuable suggestions. I also wish to acknowledge the following colleagues and friends who generously agreed to review my manuscript: Ian Alger, Ramon Greenberg, Milton Kramer, Wayne Myers, Stanley Palombo, and Robert Morton. I am most appreciative of my editor, Arthur Pomponio, who guided the book's publication from start to finish. In addition, I wish to thank Molly Ahearn for her copyediting skills, which made this book possible. Lastly, but most importantly, I could not have persevered and completed this project without the love, patience, and support of my wife and family.

Myron L. Glucksman, M.D.

1

Introduction

This book is for clinicians and others who wish to know more about understanding and using dreams to facilitate change in the lives of their clients and themselves. Change refers to greater awareness of our inner selves, including our deepest feelings, beliefs, conflicts, wishes, and fears. It also extends to our actions, behaviors, decisions, and relationships with others. Change, then, includes both our internal and external functioning. Unlocking the meaning of dreams can provide the information necessary to bring about these changes. This book aims to demonstrate a methodical approach toward understanding the meaning of dreams and using that information to promote personal change both within and outside of the context of therapy.

HISTORY OF DREAMING

From the beginning of recorded history, dreams have fascinated ancient cultures, primitive societies, philosophers, writers, and biblical figures. For the most part, dreams were viewed as supernatural phenomena caused by visitations from God, spirits, or souls. The dream was universally accepted as a mystical experience, divinely inspired, and useful as a predictor of the future. At the turn of the last century, with the publication of *The Interpretation of Dreams* (1900), Sigmund Freud introduced the concept of the dream as a psychologically meaningful phenomenon. He observed that dreams were connected to our deepest impulses and wishes. According to Freud, these impulses were products of our instinctual, biological makeup and concerned issues of survival as well as procreation. He hypothesized that most dreams originate within the context of sexual or aggressive drives that are censored by means of various mental mechanisms employed in the dream. Because, Freud believed, this process of censorship prevented the dreamer from being awakened by such impulses or wishes, the dreamer continued to sleep; thus, Freud referred to dreams as the "guardians of sleep." Freud's concept of the dream as a censorship mechanism during sleep prevailed among psychoanalysts until mid-century.

SLEEP AND DREAM RESEARCH

Beginning in the mid-twentieth century, sleep researchers discovered that dreams occurred throughout the sleep cycle on a periodic basis (Aserinsky and Kleitman 1953; Dement and Wolpert 1958; Roffwarg et al. 1962). They originate in a region of the brain known as the pons, although there is some evidence that they may also be generated by activation of other parts of the cerebral cortex (Solms 1997, 1999). Dream imagery corresponds to rhythmic electrical excitations that spread from these foci of neuronal activation to various parts of the brain. These excitations can be correlated with changes in the electroencephalogram, as well as rapid eye movements (REMs) that occur during a portion of sleep. Neurotransmitter changes also occur, including activation of cholinergic neurons and inhibition of noradrenergic, as well as serotonergic, neurons. Dreaming (REM sleep) takes up approximately 20 to 25 percent of the total night's sleep in young adults (Hartmann 1967). Dreams occur very infrequently in the remaining portion of sleep (non-REM sleep). Extensive research has indicated that dreams are essential for mental stability (Palombo 1978; Fosshage 1983; Greenberg et al. 1992; Kramer 1993; Hobson 1988, 1999). For example, if individuals are awakened each time they dream and deprived of their dreams, they will become extremely anxious, irritable, and, in some cases, mentally disorganized (Dement 1960; Gulevich, Dement, and Johnson 1966; Greenberg, Pillard, and Pearlman 1972; Webb and Agnew 1974). Moreover, laboratory experiments have demonstrated that dreams are associated with learning new tasks and with problem solving (Pearlman 1979; Smith 1985, 1993; Smith, Lapp, and Dixon 1984; Greenberg and Pearlman 1993). Current theories of dreaming suggest that during sleep we process the day's events and experiences in order to maintain our mental homeostasis. This involves evaluating, categorizing, and storing information so that it can be used for current or future decision making and problem solving. From this perspective, dreams can be understood as mental processes that enable us to adapt constructively to our environmental challenges. Although there is some evidence to support Freud's view that dreams contain or neutralize our biological instincts, their function appears to be far more encompassing. They reliably inform us of our internal physiological and psychological states. For example, certain dreams incorporate normal physiological functions, such as the need to urinate. Others may signal a physical abnormality, such as pain or discomfort in a particular part of the body. Dreams frequently reflect intense emotions that may not always be consciously experienced. They may confront us with conflicts and dilemmas that require resolution for our sense of inner security. Sometimes, they vividly portray our relationships with others or provide us with astonishingly honest portrayals of ourselves. They may also inform us of a decision we are contemplating carrying out, even before we consciously make that decision.

Creative solutions to problems, including important discoveries, often appear first in dreams (Garfield 1995). For example, the chemist Friedrich Kekule attributed his discovery of the benzene ring to a dream. Otto Loewi, a physiologist, reported that several dreams inspired his theory concerning the chemical transmission of nervous impulses (for which he received the Nobel Prize). Many artists and writers have incorporated dream imagery into their creative work. Among the best known are William Shakespeare, Fyodor Dostoevsky, and Salvador Dali.

DREAMS AND PSYCHOTHERAPY

Dreams can provide abundant information for therapists across the entire spectrum of clinical activity (Glucksman 2001). They can utilize the dreams of their clients in order to evaluate certain aspects of personality, such as character traits, mental defenses, and mood states. Perceptions and feelings of a client toward the therapist (transference) are occasionally first brought to light in a dream. By the same token, countertransference may first become evident in the dreams of the therapist, indicating unrecognized feelings and attitudes toward the client. Moreover, the salient psychodynamics underlying a client's psychopathology may be revealed more clearly in dream content than in conscious material. Likewise, the unconscious reasons for therapeutic impasses, resistance, and negative transference may emerge through a client's dreams. Dream content may also be helpful in establishing a definitive clinical diagnosis when conscious symptoms and behavior seem confusing or ambiguous. Dreams may also inform the therapist of impending suicidality, homicidality, ego disintegration, psychosis, and acting-out behavior. Progress in treatment can be monitored over time by examining the structure and content of successive dreams. Self-confidence and a readiness to terminate therapy may also initially be reflected in a dream. Dreams, then, can provide therapists and clients with an enormous amount of information that they are not necessarily consciously aware of. The key is to access and understand this information so that it can be constructively used for the benefit of the client as well as the therapist.

DREAM IMAGERY AND INTERPRETATION

Historically, dreams were interpreted for the dreamer by someone with acknowledged expertise on the subject; for example, consider the Bible's description in Genesis of Joseph's interpretation of the pharaoh's dream in which seven lean kine ate seven fat kine, and seven thin ears of corn ate seven full ears. Joseph did not ask the pharaoh for his opinion of the dream; instead, he made his famous interpretation about seven years of plenty followed by seven years of famine. It was not until Freud (1900) introduced the concept of free association that the dreamer was asked to participate actively in dream interpretation. Free association essentially means that the dreamer spontaneously says whatever comes to mind in attempting to explore the dream. This includes past and current experiences, memories, feelings, fantasies, and wishes. As the dreamer's associations continue, certain patterns become evident that point to unresolved conflicts and problems or unfulfilled wishes. Ideally, it is the dreamer who ultimately interprets the dream, aided by questions and observations on the part of a trained listener.

It is a common misconception that a specific image or symbol has a universal meaning in all dreams. For example, a snake may not only be a phallic symbol, but it may also portray deception, sneakiness, or danger. The actual meaning of an image corresponds to the dreamer's associations with that image in terms of his or her unique past and present experience. As an example, the American flag occurring in one person's dream may symbolize a sense of patriotism and loyalty, while in another person's dream it may evoke a memory of the flag in a school classroom and be associated with feelings of nostalgia for one's early youth. Images in dreams are highly idiosyncratic, and their meanings are quite specific for each individual; moreover, the same image may change its meaning from one dream to another for the same person. An image or group of images may reflect a theme, conflict, or problem connected to one or more events and feelings. Freud termed this phenomenon *condensation*. For example, an image of a person struggling to climb up a hill may reflect the dreamer's feelings of depression, along with difficulty in carrying out daily activities. The image of a shark loose in an office building may portray the dreamer's anxiety at work in connection with a coworker's competitiveness and hostility. Several juxtaposed images may portray a more complex story; for example, a dreamer sees her childhood home surrounded by a gray mist. There is no one else around. Then she finds herself walking out of a dark cave holding a little girl in her arms. Based on the dreamer's associations, these images represent a condensation of the dreamer's recollections of her childhood experience, including feeling lonely, without friends, and a lack of affection from her parents. The little girl represents her inner sense of isolation and emotional impoverishment resulting from her upbringing. Carrying the child out of the cave reflects her current attempt to change those aspects of herself through therapy. Another dreamer is in a swimming race that she is winning. Suddenly, a man holds her head under water so that she is unable to breathe and is prevented from winning the race. The dreamer's associations indicate that these images are connected to her desire to complete an important project at work, which, if successful, will lead to a promotion. However, she has a work block and keeps procrastinating. A contributing factor is her lack of self-confidence, which she attributes to her father's repeated devaluation of her achievements (the man holding her head under water). These examples illustrate how condensation (an image or group of images) can portray in symbolic shorthand a problem or conflict, along with past or present circumstances and feelings connected to it.

Sometimes, an image, such as a place or person, may represent something or someone entirely different. In other words, it is a substitute image, or *displacement*. For example, a woman dreams that she is dancing with President Eisenhower. She associates this to her relationship with her male therapist, whom she views as possessing certain characteristics of Eisenhower (e.g., he is a leader who can be firm and self-confident, yet gentle and folksy). A young man dreams that he is watching a tiger leap through the air. The tiger's power, grace, and sure-footedness are qualities he wishes for himself as an athlete. Another dreamer finds herself in a garden full of beautiful flowers. The garden and the scent of the flowers remind her of her mother, who wore a particular perfume when she was a child. She is filled with feelings of happiness and love when she recollects her closeness with her mother at that time in her life.

It is not uncommon for past and present events to be included in the imagery of the same dream. This phenomenon is most likely related to the information-processing and storage function of dreaming. *Day residue* is a term that refers to the imagery in a dream connected to the previous day's events. Contemporary theories of dreaming hypothesize that current experiences are matched and stored in the brain's memory systems, which contain similar experiences from the past. These past and present experiences are processed along with the emotions, thoughts, and behavior associated with them. If a current problem or conflict is being addressed, past solutions and adaptive behaviors are applied or modified in order to resolve the current issue. According to M. F. Reiser (2001), current life experience may be matched with past memories through affects that are connected to them by the current conflict or situation. This matching function can be considered "off-line processing" that has survival value for both animals and humans (Dewan 1970; Winson 1985). An example of this is the dream of a divorced female executive afraid of losing her job because her company was downsizing. Moreover, she was in an unhappy romantic relationship with a married man. She dreamed that she was riding on a bus in California that was traveling in the wrong direction. She eventually got off and found a bus going in the opposite direction. Soon after having this dream, she was able to secure her position at work and broke off her unsatisfactory relationship. Her associations included the fact that she had lived and worked in California shortly after her divorce. During that period of her life, she felt independent, happy, and secure in her career. She resolved to duplicate that experience and took the necessary steps to change her job status as well as her unsatisfactory relationship. This dream illustrates the influence of past experience on current decision making.

Sometimes, a constructive resolution cannot be reached, and the dreamer is left feeling anxious and uncertain. If the anxiety develops into frank terror, the dreamer may be awakened from what is commonly termed a *nightmare*. For example, a woman dreamed that while she was crossing a bridge, a storm developed with high winds. The bridge began to collapse, and she awoke as she was falling into the water. The dream occurred while she was making a major transition in her life, and she was afraid of failing. The collapse of the bridge symbolized her dread of the consequences of failure.

DREAMWORK

Freud believed that the major purpose of dreaming was to suppress or contain the various impulses and wishes that we consciously or unconsciously harbor. According to Freud, these wishes and impulses became activated during sleep and, if not censored, might arouse the dreamer to the point of waking up. Freud hypothesized that certain mechanisms, which he referred to as *dreamwork*, censored or neutralized these wishes and impulses in order to maintain the sleeping state of the dreamer. Symbolism, condensation, and displacement were first described by Freud as constituting the essential mechanisms of dreamwork. He referred to the images in the dream that reflect these censoring mechanisms as the *manifest content*. The actual wishes and impulses that have been disguised or censored are termed the *latent content*. Free association to the imagery of the manifest content leads the dreamer to the latent content. The manifest content may be further distorted and forgotten by means of *secondary revision* once the dreamer awakens. Accurate recall of the manifest content can be accomplished in the sleep laboratory by awakening the dreamer when rapid eye movements and the electroencephalogram indicate that dreaming is taking place.

Contemporary dream investigators believe that the manifest content is not so much a censoring mechanism as it is a metaphorical portrayal of the issues and conflicts being addressed in the dream (Bonime 1962 [1982]; Fosshage 1987; Hill 1996; Blechner 2001). According to this viewpoint, rather than functioning as elements of disguise, symbolism, condensation, and displacement are the key components of the metaphorical language of the dream and require interpretation. Although some believe that dream imagery is random, without psychodynamic meaning (Hobson and McCarley 1977), most clinicians are impressed with the relevance of dreams to psychic functioning. Conceptualizing dream imagery as a metaphorical narrative is analogous to understanding the underlying meaning of an abstract painting. Inevitably, it is the dreamer's associations that provide the raw data for an ultimate understanding of the dream. Unless the dreamer is awakened during REM sleep in the laboratory, a distortion or loss of the actual manifest content usually occurs. This raises questions as to the accuracy of dream interpretation based on the dreamer's recollection of the manifest content. While there is no clear solution to this problem, most clinicians would agree that what the dreamer does recall, or even distorts, is of significance. Moreover, a dream may lend itself to more than one interpretation based on the dreamer's associations. Even in the absence of interpretation, the associations connected to the dream may lead to important observations and insights. Therefore, the accuracy of the dreamer's recollection of the manifest content is of less importance than the meaning and insight that may ultimately be derived from the manifest content. Although many dreams can never be fully understood, their imagery may nevertheless lead us to greater knowledge of our clients, ourselves, and the world around us.

The main purpose of this book is to demonstrate how understanding and applying the meaning of dreams can help us change various aspects of our self-awareness, functioning, and behavior. It is meant for therapists, clients, and others who are interested in working with dreams. Among the subjects to be addressed are free association, emotions, self-identity, relationships with others, decision making and problem solving, life crises and stress, physical and emotional trauma, anxiety and repetitive dreams, wish-fulfillment dreams, changes in dream content over time, the interpretive process, and the use of dreams as facilitators of change during psychotherapy and through self-interpretation. Examples throughout the book explain how dreams can be understood and interpreted in order to help the dreamer bring about internal and external change. Particular emphasis is placed on the use of dreams during psychotherapy in order to promote greater self-awareness, insight, and change.

REFERENCES

Aserinsky, E., and N. Kleitman. 1953. Regularly occurring periods of ocular motility and concomitant phenomena during sleep. *Science* 118:361–75.

Blechner, M. J. 2001. *The dream frontier*. Hillsdale, NJ: The Analytic Press.

Bonime, W., with F. Bonime. 1962 [1982]. *The clinical use of dreams*. New York: Basic Books and DeCapo Press.

Dement, W. 1960. The effect of dream deprivation. *Science* 131:1705–1707.

Dement, W., and E. Wolpert. 1958. The relation of eye movements, body motility, and external stimuli to dream content. *J. of Experimental Psychology* 55:543–53.

Dewan, E. M. 1970. The programming (P) hypothesis for REM sleep. In *Sleep and dreaming*, ed. E. Hartmann, 295–307. Boston: Little, Brown.

Fosshage, J. 1983. The psychological function of dreams: A revised psychoanalytic perspective. *Psychoanalysis and Contemporary Thought* 6, no. 4:641–69.

———. 1987. New vistas in dream interpretation. In *Dreams in new perspective: The royal road revisited*, ed. M. Glucksman and S. L. Warner, 23–43. New York: Human Sciences Press.

Freud, S. 1900 [1958]. The interpretation of dreams. In *The standard edition of the complete psychological works of Sigmund Freud*, ed. and trans. J. Strachey. Vols. 4 and 5. London: Hogarth Press.

Garfield, P. L. 1995. *Creative dreaming*. New York: Simon and Schuster.

Glucksman, M. L. 2001. The dream: A psychodynamically informative instrument. *J. of Psychotherapy Practice and Research* 10, no. 4:223–30.

Greenberg, R., H. Katz, W. Schwartz, and C. Pearlman. 1992. A research-based reconsideration of psychoanalytic dream theory. *J. of the American Psychoanalytic Association* 40:531–50.

Greenberg, R., and C. Pearlman. 1993. An integrated approach to dream theory: Contributions from sleep research and clinical practice. In *The functions of dreaming*, ed. A. Moffitt, M. Kramer, and R. Hoffmann, 363–80. Albany: State University of New York Press.

Greenberg, R., R. Pillard, and C. Pearlman. 1972. The effect of dream deprivation on adaptation to stress. *Psychosomatic Medicine* 34:257–62.

Gulevich, G., W. C. Dement, and L. Johnson. 1966. Psychiatric and EEG observations on a case of prolonged (264 h) wakefulness. *Archives of General Psychiatry* 15:29–35.

Hartmann, E. 1967. *The biology of dreaming*. Springfield, IL: Charles C. Thomas.

Hill, C. E. 1996. *Working with dreams in psychotherapy*. New York: Guilford Press.

Hobson, J. A., and R. W. McCarley. 1977. The brain as a dream-state generator: An activation-synthesis hypothesis of the dream process. *American J. of Psychiatry* 34:1335–48.

Hobson, J. A. 1988. *The dreaming brain*. New York: Basic Books.

———. 1999. The new neuropsychology of sleep: Implications for psychoanalysis. *Neuro-Psychoanalysis* 1, no. 2:157–83.

Kramer, M. 1993. The selective mood regulatory function of dreaming: An update and revision. In *The functions of dreaming*, ed. A. Moffitt, M. Kramer, and R. Hoffmann, 139–95. Albany: State University of New York Press.

Oxford Study Bible. 1992. Genesis 41:1–4. *Revised English Bible*. New York: Oxford University Press.

Palombo, S. R. 1978. *Dreaming and memory*. New York: Basic Books.

Pearlman, C. 1979. REM sleep and information processing: Evidence from animal studies. *Neuroscience and Biobehavioral Reviews* 3:57–68.

Reiser, M. F. 2001. The dream in contemporary psychiatry. *American J. of Psychiatry* 158:351–59.

Roffwarg, H., W. Dement, T. Muzio, and C. Fisher. 1962. Dream imagery: Relationship to rapid eye movements. *Archives of General Psychiatry* 7:235–38.

Smith, C. 1985. Sleep states and learning: A review of the animal literature. *Neuroscience and Biobehavioral Reviews* 9:157–68.

———. 1993. REM sleep and learning: Some recent findings. In *The functions of dreaming*, ed. A. Moffitt, M. Kramer, and R. Hoffmann, 341–62, Albany: State University of New York Press.

Smith, C., L. Lapp, and M. Dixon. 1984. Increased REM density following major learning experiences in humans. *Sleep Research* 13:99.

Solms, M. 1997. *The neuropsychology of dreams: A clinico-anatomical study*. Mahwah, NJ: Lawrence Erlbaum.

———. 1999. Commentary on the new neuropsychology of sleep: Implications for psychoanalysis. *Neuro-Psychoanalysis* 1, no. 2:183–95.

Winson, J. 1985. Brain and psyche: The biology of the unconscious. New York: Doubleday/Anchor Press.

Webb, W. B. and H. W. Agnew, Jr. 1974. The effects of a chronic limitation of sleep length. *Psychophysiology*. 11: 265-274.

SUGGESTED READING

Abrams, D. M. 1992. The dreamer's mirror of reality. *Contemporary Psychoanalysis* 23:50–71.

Alston, T. M., R. C. Calogeras, and H. Deserno, eds. 1993. *Dream reader: Psychoanalytic articles on dreams*. Madison, CT: International Universities Press.

Caligor, L., and R. May. 1963. *Dreams and symbols*. New York: Basic Books.

Cartwright, R. D. 1977. *Night life: Explorations in dreaming*. Engelwood Cliffs, NJ: Prentice Hall.

Epstein, A. W. 1995. *Dreaming and other involuntary mentation: An essay on neuropsychiatry*. Madison, CT: International Universities Press.

Fosshage, J. 1997. The organizing functions of dream mentation. *Contemporary Psychoanalysis* 33:429–58.

Freud, S. 1933[1958]. Revision of the theory of dreams. In *The standard edition of the complete psychological works of Sigmund Freud*, ed. and trans. J. Strachey, Vol. 22, 7–30. London: Hogarth Press.

Hall, C. 1966. *The meaning of dreams*. New York: McGraw-Hill.

Hartmann, E. 1973. *The functions of sleep*. New Haven, CT: Yale University Press.

Lansky, M. R., ed. 1992. *Essential papers on dreams*. New York: New York University Press.

Natterson, J. M., ed. 1980. *The dream in clinical practice*. New York: Jason Aronson.

Sloane, P. 1979. *Psychoanalytic understanding of the dream*. New York: Jason Aronson.

Winson, J. 1990. The meaning of dreams. *Scientific American* 263:86–96.

Woods, R. L., and H. B. Greenhouse, eds. 1974. *The new world of dreams*. New York: MacMillan Publishing Co.

2

Free Association and Interpretation

In order for dreams to be used advantageously, it is essential to understand the meaning underlying the manifest content, that is, the latent content. The time-honored approach to deciphering the latent meaning of dreams has been free association (Freud 1900). Literally speaking, free association means that the dreamer verbalizes or writes down spontaneously occurring thoughts, fantasies, images, memories, or feelings evoked by the dream imagery. In the treatment setting, this is done in the presence of a trained therapist, who can listen to the client's verbal productions and help organize them into a meaningful narrative. However, this process is not a one-way street; rather, it is a mutual interaction between the client and the therapist. That is, the client's free associations inevitably evoke questions by the therapist, leading to further associations and more requests for elaboration and clarification. Through this collaborative effort, the client and the therapist arrive at a mutual understanding of the dream. In this context, interpretation is ideally the result of a cooperative effort arrived at by consensus (Bonime 1986). However, when the client is alone, without the assistance of a trained listener, unraveling the meaning of the dream presents an even greater challenge. Nevertheless, both client and therapist can employ a methodical approach toward achieving an interpretation of the dream inside or outside of the therapy setting.

DREAM RECALL

The first step in dream interpretation is to recall the dream. Clients are more likely to recall or think about their dreams if the therapist orients them to the significance of dreams in their lives. Continued encouragement and questioning about dreams during therapy can be helpful. Sometimes, clients minimize the importance of their dreams by saying, "It's only a dream. It's not real." Therapists can respond by emphasizing that dreams are a genuine inner experience that may have significant meaning for the client. At the time of awakening, most or all dreams are forgotten. The dreams most likely to be remembered are either anxiety dreams (nightmares) or those that occur shortly before awakening. Often, the dreamer is left with only an image or a fragment of an image upon awakening. It is important to keep in mind that even single or partial images are worthwhile noting. The most effective ways to remember dreams include writing down or tape-recording the recollected imagery upon awakening. Otherwise, dream content will inevitably be forgotten. Even the most experienced person who works with dreams will forget a significant amount of the manifest content over the course of the succeeding day. Once the dream is written or recorded, the following components of the manifest content can be examined in order to understand it.

Theme(s) of the Dream

Most dreams have a central topic or theme, even if it is only an image. Consider, for example, a dreamer who awoke with an image of being attacked by a swarm of bees. The obvious theme was that of being under attack. A related theme was that of being stung or hurt. Since the manifest content can be considered a metaphorical presentation, it is necessary to think about the image in figurative, rather than literal, terms. A useful technique is to associate how the theme applies to one's present or past life. In this case, the dreamer associated to a hurtful remark made by her mother-in-law. The latter reminded her of a "busy bee," or someone who is intrusive and meddlesome. The remark "stung" the dreamer because it was critical and insensitive.

A man dreamed that he was playing on a basketball team and scored baskets frequently. His teammates always passed the ball to him, making it easy for him to take shots. The theme of this dream was about being effective and successful. A related theme was that of being helped and supported. The man associated to his work and the fact that he was enjoying some recent successes. Moreover, he attributed his accomplishments to the helpfulness and cooperativeness of his coworkers.

Another man dreamed that a plane was attempting to take off but couldn't lift off the runway. The theme of this dream was procrastination and the inability to complete a task. The man associated to the fact that he was unable to complete a project at work because he lacked adequate information and was afraid of being criticized. Procrastination protected him from the possibility of criticism and failure.

A woman dreamed that she was driving a car down a hill when the brakes failed. The car began accelerating and went out of control. She fully anticipated crashing and being killed but woke up before it happened. The theme of this dream was loss of control with a fatal outcome. In this case, the dreamer was becoming involved in a romantic relationship and felt that she was falling in love. However, she had a history of failed relationships and was afraid that that this relationship would also end disastrously. Sometimes, themes are not obvious or recognizable, and other elements need to be analyzed in order to understand the dream.

Feelings and Mood

Many dreams contain feelings or emotions that are readily identifiable. Others may express feelings in a more symbolic fashion. For example, a woman dreamed that she was swimming in a stormy sea, and the waves were growing larger and larger. She realized that no one was around to rescue her and that she was going to drown. She became terrified and felt totally helpless. In this instance, the dreamer associated to a feeling of intense rage that she believed was about to overwhelm her. In addition, she felt alone, without anyone in whom she could confide or who could offer her help. Her rage was self-directed, and she was afraid that she would act on her suicidal fantasies. In this dream, the ever larger waves symbolically represented her mounting rage. On the other hand, she also directly experienced her feelings of terror and helplessness in the dream.

A man dreamed that he had killed somebody, but no one knew about it. He felt extremely guilty in the dream and was afraid of being discovered as the murderer. His associations led to guilt feelings about harboring death wishes toward a professional associate. The dreamer was unaware of these feelings, and his conscious fantasies of wishing his partner dead had been fleeting and totally forgotten until he had the dream. This is a good example of how feelings are often repressed or forgotten, but then surface in a dream.

A woman dreamed that she was walking alone on a very cold day. There was an icy wind that froze her through her clothing. She associated to her unhappy marriage and her husband's emotional remoteness. She longed for love and intimacy but felt only emotional coldness and emptiness. In this case, the icy wind and freezing temperature symbolically represented her relationship with her husband as well as her internal emotional state.

Another woman dreamed that she was at a country fair and saw a bunch of colorful balloons floating in the air. They were her favorite colors: red, yellow, and blue. She was in a happy and buoyant mood. The dream reminded her of a childhood experience when her parents took her to the circus. She recalled that her mother wore a colorful dress containing the same colors as the balloons. It was a happy event during which she felt secure and loved by her parents. Her parents later divorced, and a series of tragic events occurred in her life. Her dream symbolically and experientially represented her wish to recapture the feelings she had as a child prior to the unhappy events of her adulthood.

A current theory of dream function is that emotions are processed and regulated during dreaming (Kramer 1993). For example, intense negative feelings, such as anger, fear, guilt, and sadness, are often expressed and then neutralized in the course of dreaming. On the other hand, positive feelings, such as joy, elation, and sexual arousal, can also be experienced in dreams. Current research indicates that emotions are almost always present in the manifest content of dreams or in the associative material (Kramer and Glucksman 2006). The feelings that occur during dreaming are often predictive of the mood of the dreamer on the following day. As an example, if excessive sadness in a dream is not somehow resolved or dissipated, the dreamer may awaken the following day in a sad mood. Conversely, if a dream is predominantly happy, the dreamer will most likely be in a good mood the following day. A lack of feelings during dreaming is also significant. This may indicate that the dreamer is denying specific feelings or lacks the capacity to experience feelings altogether. Certain pathological conditions, such as dissociation and alexithymia, are characterized by a paucity or absence of emotional content in dreams. By and large, identifying feelings in dream material is an important avenue toward understanding the meaning of a dream. Chapter 3, "Emotions or Feelings, and Mood," will elaborate on how to identify and constructively use feelings that occur in dreams.

Context and Surroundings

It is important to pay attention to context and the surrounding landscape in dreams. This means that both the external environment and inner psychological state in which the dream occurs may have significance. For example, a woman dreamed that she found herself outside her childhood home. However, there was a gray mist all around her, and she had difficulty visualizing her house. It became apparent that she had forgotten significant portions of her childhood until mid-adolescence. The gray mist and her visual difficulty symbolized her amnesia concerning much of her childhood.

A man dreamed that he was a soldier and part of Hitler's entourage on a battlefield with many trenches. He was engaged in bloody hand-to-hand combat. His associations to the battlefield and Hitler reminded him of his childhood relationship with his father, who was punitive and a strict disciplinarian. They had many arguments, some leading to violent confrontations during which his father beat him.

A woman who had been sexually abused by her father dreamed that she observed a man and a little girl sitting on a pile of wood. Her associations led to memories of being sexually abused by her father in their basement, where a lot of lumber was piled up. Subsequently, similar dreams and their associations confirmed the childhood sexual abuse that she did not consciously recall.

A man dreamed that he was ripping up the floorboards in the house where he grew up. Suddenly, he found a confederate flag hidden under the boards. He was born and raised in the South but had spent the better part of his life in a northern city. He was at a stage in therapy where he was recollecting his childhood and some of the formative influences that had shaped his personality. Exploring underneath the floor and finding the confederate flag represented his journey into his Southern upbringing, as well as his discovery of key experiences that formed his identity.

A woman dreamed about a beautiful garden with flowers that were especially fragrant. Her associations led to memories of her mother's perfume when she was a child, prior to her mother's hospitalization for mental illness. This led to a prolonged separation from her mother and a loss of the close attachment and security she felt prior to her mother's absence. The fragrance of the flowers represented her mother's perfume and the close bond she felt with, and the love she felt for, her mother.

Some dreams are noteworthy for the absence of surroundings and people in their manifest content. Often, these are the dreams of individuals who are socially isolated and withdrawn. Sometimes, they may be indicative of a person who lacks an inner identity or suffers from emotional emptiness. For example, a woman had a series of dreams in which she found herself totally alone on a deserted island in the middle of an ocean. She had been sexually and emotionally traumatized as a child and learned to protect herself from the painful feelings connected with these experiences by emotionally numbing herself. Consequently, she was unable to sense or describe her inner feelings and lacked a cohesive self-identity. As a result, she felt emotionally isolated and detached from others. As these examples illustrate, the contextual elements of a dream contain vital information that may lead to a clearer understanding of the dream's meaning.

Activity and Behavior

Most dreams contain some kind of activity or behavior on the part of the dreamer or other persons and objects. For example, a man dreamed that he was swimming and fishing at the same time. He was catching so many fish that he felt overwhelmed and unable to handle them all. His associations led to his current business activities, which he felt were more than he could cope with effectively.

A woman dreamed that she was watching the creation of the world from its primary elements. She saw the oceans, land, lakes, mountains, and rivers being formed. It was an indescribable process that she observed with great awe. At the time of the dream, she was about to finish writing a book, a project that had taken several years, and she was amazed that she had been able to complete it. In addition, she was perplexed, as well as grateful, about how she had been able to create and finish such a complex piece of work.

A man dreamed that he was traveling along a road until he came to a fork. He knew that he had to decide to take one direction or the other. He was unable to make up his mind. The dreamer was unhappily married and involved in a relationship with another woman. She was pressuring him to divorce his wife and marry her. He was ambivalent about doing so because of conflicted feelings toward the other woman, as well as a previous failed marriage.

A woman dreamed that she was bleeding profusely from her vagina all over the floor and was busily trying to clean it up. Shortly before the dream, she had had an abortion in the context of a serious illness and an unhappy marriage. She felt guilty about the abortion but knew that she could not have more children until she was well again and had improved her marriage. Her interpretation was that she had to "clean up" her life before she could consider another pregnancy.

A man had repetitive dreams of being chased by other men with knives or guns. He usually escaped, but sometimes they would capture and torture him by cutting off his finger or other limbs. The dreamer's father, a doctor, was physically and psychologically abusive. When the dreamer was eight years old, his father performed a tonsillectomy on him. It was a terrifying experience, especially being anesthetized with an ether mask. As a teenager, he slept with a knife under his pillow because he was afraid his father might actually try to kill him. Understandably, he was extremely distrustful and frightened of other men. Although all of these dreams contain emotional, as well as other elements, the activity and behavior of people and objects in them reflect their essential dynamics.

People and Relationships

Individuals, as well as their relationships, are sources of important data in the manifest content of dreams. As pointed out in chapter 1, the appearance of a particular person may not necessarily be a literal representation of that individual. Rather, individuals are often substitutes for, or displacements of, others who are meaningful to the dreamer. For example, a woman who had just begun therapy dreamed that she was in church confessing to a kindly priest. It became apparent from her associations that the priest represented her male therapist, whom she felt was an empathic listener. Moreover, she felt guilty about some of the material she was discussing with him, and wished to be forgiven.

A man dreamed that while he was visiting a friend, he looked out the window and saw a stranger get in his car, drive off, and then smash it into another car. He ran out and confronted the stranger, but the man said he was only trying to park it and refused to apologize. When he returned to his friend, the latter had disappeared. The dreamer felt abused, betrayed, and rejected. His associations revealed that he had developed a deep mistrust of others, particularly men, because of his abusive, critical father. He continually anticipated hurt, rejection, or indifference in his relationships with men.

A woman dreamed that she was at a party with members of the chorus in which she sang. However, the party was being held at the house where she had lived while in high school. She felt unwelcome and sensed that the other guests were uninterested in what she had to say. She left the party feeling excluded and rejected. The dreamer had, in fact, belonged to a chorus in high school, where she had felt shy and unpopular. She experienced similar feelings when she was with members of her present chorus, as well as with others in general. The source of her social discomfort then, as now, was her fear of saying something stupid or wrong, for which she would be criticized and ostracized.

A young man in treatment for multiple phobias and anxiety dreamed that he was floating in a rowboat with his male therapist. Suddenly, a huge menacing sea monster rose up in front of them. His therapist calmly guided the boat around the monster until they were in safe waters again. The patient associated the monster to his father, who was a physically imposing man, as well as loud and frightening. His phobias and anxiety were largely connected to his fear of his father. However, he experienced his therapist as quietly strong, comforting, and helpful. He attributed his improvement in treatment to his relationship with his therapist, who was quite different from his father. Floating in the rowboat with his therapist represented the therapeutic journey.

A woman who was sexually inhibited and insecure with men dreamed that she was making love with her boyfriend when a Japanese woman suddenly jumped through the window and attacked her. She associated to her mother, who was a painter and had spent considerable time in Japan studying art. Her parents were divorced, and her mother repeatedly told her daughter how bitter she was toward her father. Moreover, she continually warned her that men were untrustworthy and hurtful. The dream informed her of how influential her mother was in deterring her from enjoying and committing herself to romantic relationships with men.

The foregoing examples illustrate how important it is to observe the behavioral qualities of individuals, as well as the nature of relationships in dreams.

Portrayals of Self

Since dreams are the products or creations of the dreamer, their content may reflect different aspects of the self. However, certain dreams, in particular, focus on the self or specific characteristics of the self. These types of dreams are referred to as *self-state dreams* (Kohut 1977; Ornstein 1987). For example, a man who was beginning therapy dreamed that he had an incurable brain tumor. His associations led to his conviction that the personality difficulties that had brought him to treatment were not changeable.

A woman being treated for a malignancy dreamed that she was dying in the hospital, surrounded by friends and family. She felt content and at peace, knowing that she was cared for and loved. In reality, her treatment had been successful, but she was nevertheless afraid of dying from a possible recurrence. She hoped that if her disease turned out to be fatal, she would die with the knowledge that her life had been fulfilling and that her family and friends had loved her.

A man was receiving an important promotion at work. He was anxious about whether or not he could perform successfully at it. In this context, he dreamed that he was playing in a football game. The quarterback threw a pass to him, which he caught for a touchdown. He felt exhilarated and confident after having the dream. His self-image in the dream portrayed his wish to be competent and successful in the new job.

A woman dreamed that she was cradling a baby girl in her arms. She felt that the baby was a part of herself that required protection and soothing. Her parents had been emotionally distant and unaffectionate. In addition, her husband was excessively critical and abusive. She wished that she could relive her life and receive the love and nurturing she missed.

Sometimes, the self is displaced in dreams, either onto another person or onto an animal, or object. For example, a woman dreamed that she saw a two-headed pig. One head of the pig was very cute and sweet, while the other was ugly and mean looking. The two heads reminded her of contrasting parts of herself; sometimes, she could be charming and pleasant, while at other times she was greedy and nasty.

A woman who had spent most of her adult life in a convent and was still a virgin considered leaving it and beginning a heterosexual life. She dreamed that she was in a museum looking at a statue of a unicorn that was on a necklace. The unicorn is a mythical animal with a horn on its forehead and thought to symbolize chastity and purity. It reminded her of her ambivalence about giving up her celibacy and becoming heterosexually active, which was a major conflict for her at that time. These examples demonstrate that dreams of the self can either be direct or take the form of displacements, animate or inanimate. They are highly informative regarding perceptions, attitudes, wishes, and feelings pertaining to the self.

In summary, dreams can be understood and interpreted by means of free association, using a methodical process. This involves examining the manifest content according to the following components: theme(s), feelings or mood, context and surroundings, activity and behavior, people and relationships, and portrayals or images of the self. Free association entails focusing as spontaneously as possible on past and present events, memories, thoughts, fantasies, wishes, and feelings, keeping the previous components in mind. For purposes of remembering and free associating to dreams, especially for those who are beginning this process, it is best to write down or record the manifest content, as well as the associations to it.

The following is an example of a dream and the dreamer's spontaneous free associations to it:

> I was on a subway station platform near the end of the line. I swung my arm and accidentally knocked off my glasses. They landed on the track, and I wanted to retrieve them. I stepped onto the tracks to get them, but was concerned about the third rail being live. I saw an opening between the tracks and stepped through it to get my glasses. There was a train coming, so I quickly grabbed my glasses and went through the opening again. I made it back to the platform.

The dreamer's free associations were as follows:

> I actually did accidentally drop my umbrella onto the subway tracks about twenty years ago. I retrieved it without getting electrocuted. I was married to my first wife at the time. I didn't know then what was in store for me—divorce, job changes—maybe not having my glasses on meant I couldn't see what was coming in my life. The day before I had the dream, I presented my department's budget and plans for the coming year to my boss. He was critical and actually rejected it. I don't think there's a future for me with the company. I'm really scared and think I should send out my resume in order to find another job. I called Diane the other day and asked her if she wanted to spend Christmas with me. She said it would be best if we didn't see each other. She's probably right. It would be a mistake for me to get involved with her again—she's too volatile and unpredictable. I guess I need to find another job and another girlfriend, but it's scary. Maybe that's what the dream is about.

The dreamer was a divorced man who was having difficulty in his career and his relationships with women. The theme of the dream centered on his need to reestablish a secure job and a more stable relationship with a woman. The predominant feeling was fear of failing in both endeavors. The context was a potentially dangerous situation: that is, losing his job and returning to a troubled relationship. His activity in the dream enabled him to retrieve his glasses and to avoid the oncoming train. In other words, the underlying wish was to find another job and a more suitable girlfriend. Although he was the only person in the manifest content of the dream, his associations included his former wife, girlfriend, and boss. His portrayal of self in the dream was of someone who was decisive and able to take action and succeed. In retrospect, this was a decision-making dream because he ultimately left his job and began a relationship with another woman.

Therapists who are exploring a dream with a client can benefit from referring to the various components of the manifest content in order to help the dreamer free-associate to it. Questions and observations pertaining to the different elements of the manifest content may be necessary. For example, clients should be encouraged to elaborate on the feelings they experience in their dreams. Likewise, people, surroundings, places, objects, behaviors, activities, and colors can be focused on and pursued with the dreamer. Past memories and experiences, as well as current events and circumstances, should also be kept in mind. However, it is extremely important for therapists to encourage associations from the dreamer rather than introducing their own. Sometimes, a client's associations may remind the therapist of a relevant experience or event in the client's life. In this instance, the therapist may choose to bring up this material with the intent of helping the client make further connections. In rare circumstances, the therapist may offer a personal association that is relevant and appropriate to the client's associative stream. However, this must be done judiciously, without introducing the therapist's issues or conflicts into the dialogue. Hopefully, free association leads to the mutual interpretation and understanding of a dream by both client and therapist. However, when the client arrives at an interpretation independently of the therapist, it has a much more powerful impact on the client because self-interpretation reflects his or her autonomous observations about a unique, self-created inner drama. If it becomes necessary for the therapist to offer an interpretation, this is best done tentatively, with as much participation by the client as possible. It is important to keep in mind that interpretation is not necessarily the primary or exclusive goal of free association. Of greater importance are the insights and connections that associations may evoke. In this sense, the dream really serves as a stimulus or starting point for an in-depth exploration of the self. Eventually, self-introspection and self-interpretation can be accomplished after a considerable amount of practice using the associative process. Free association in the context of therapy, mutual therapist-client interpretation, and self-interpretation are addressed in chapter 11, "The Interpretive Process."

The following are suggested steps for therapists and clients to take in order to free-associate to dream manifest content:

1. Write down or record the manifest content of the dream as soon as possible after awaking from it. Images, fragments of imagery, and any other recollections of the dream are important to note.
2. Associate as spontaneously as possible to various components of the manifest content, including themes, feelings, moods, surroundings, activities, behaviors, people, relationships, and self.
3. Attempt to connect each element of the manifest content to current and past events, memories, fantasies, wishes, conflicts, and problems.
4. Focus as much as possible on unusual or striking imagery (e.g., colors, bizarre behaviors or events, objects, people, and places).
5. Therapists should encourage clients to elaborate in as much detail as possible on various components of the imagery. Associations or observations on the part of the therapist should be introduced sparingly and judiciously.
6. Remember that interpretation is not necessarily the primary goal of free association. Connections, insights, and new perspectives are equally important.
7. If an interpretation is reached, it is best arrived at by the client. Interpretation by the therapist should be tentative and open-ended so that the client can continue to reflect on it.
8. Self-interpretation, as well as greater insight and understanding by the client, are the ultimate goals of the associative process.

REFERENCES

Bonime, W. 1986. Collaborative dream interpretation. *J. of the American Academy of Psychoanalysis* 14, no. 1:15–26.

Freud, S. 1900 [1958]. The interpretation of dreams. In *The standard edition of the complete psychological works of Sigmund Freud*, ed. and trans. J. Strachey. Vols. 4 and 5. London: Hogarth Press.

Kohut, H. 1977. *The restoration of the self*. New York: International Universities Press.

Kramer, M. 1993. The selective mood regulatory function of dreaming: An update and revision. In *The functions of dreaming*, ed. A. Moffitt, M. Kramer, and R. Hoffmann, 139–95. Albany: State University of New York Press.

Kramer, M., and M. L. Glucksman. 2006. Changes in manifest dream affect during psychoanalytic treatment. *Journal of the American Academy of Psychoanalysis and Dynamic Psychiatry* 34, no. 2:249–60.

Ornstein, P. H. 1987. On self-state dreams in the psychoanalytic treatment process. In *The interpretations of dreams in clinical work*, ed. A. Rothstein. Monograph 3, 87–104. Madison, CT: International Universities Press.

SUGGESTED READING

Greenson, R. R. 1970. The exceptional position of the dream in psychoanalytic practice. *Psychoanalytic Quarterly* 39:519–49.

Gutheil, E. A. 1951. *The handbook of dream analysis.* New York: Liveright Publishing.

Hill, C. E. 1996. *Working with dreams in psychotherapy.* New York: The Guilford Press.

Reiser, M. F. 1990. *Memory in mind and brain: What dream imagery reveals.* New York: Basic Books.

Sloane, P. 1979. *Psychoanalytic understanding of the dream.* New York: Jason Aronson.

Weiss, L. 1986. *Dream analysis in psychotherapy.* New York: Pergamon Press.

3

Emotions or Feelings, and Mood

DEFINITION

In order to discuss the role of emotions or feelings, and mood in dreams, it is important to understand the meanings of these terms. *Emotions* and *feelings* are synonymous and refer to an internal psychological state, as well as a physiological response. For example, fear is a distinct sensation characterized by the perception of extreme apprehension, rapid heart rate, and bodily tension. Sadness is characterized by unhappiness, diminished alertness, and frequent tearfulness. Joy is a pleasurable, euphoric state often accompanied by laughter and physical relaxation. Emotions are mediated by brain centers, including the amygdala and limbic system, which have connections to other parts of the brain. These, in turn, regulate changes in brain neurotransmitters, hormones, and that part of the nervous system (autonomic) that controls the internal organs (heart, gastrointestinal tract) and skeletal musculature (voluntary nervous system). Therefore, emotions are intimately connected to other mental functions (cognition, perception, memory), as well as to physiological processes (movement, sensation, heart rate). Emotions, or feelings, are usually transient, lasting from minutes to hours. *Mood* refers to one or more emotions that may last from hours to days. Therefore, one can be happy or sad for minutes or days. *Affect* is an inclusive term that refers to feelings or emotions, or mood. If a mood persists for an excessive period, it may become pathological. For example, prolonged sadness may evolve into clinical depression. On the other hand, continuous joy or euphoria may develop into a manic state. Emotions and moods are governed largely by events, experiences, thoughts, fantasies, and memories. They are vital components of interpersonal communication in the same way that language is. In fact, verbal and emotional forms of expression proceed hand in glove, much like lyrics and melody in a song. If someone says he or she feels happy in a somber tone of voice, the communication is confusing and clearly not one of distinct happiness. However, if that person claims happiness and is smiling, the verbal and physical communications are consistent. Therefore, although emotions are subjectively experienced, they can be objectively appreciated to some extent.

EMOTIONAL DEVELOPMENT

Although all humans are born with the capacity to experience feelings, they nevertheless need to be taught how to recognize and express them. J. Panksepp (1998, 1999, 2001) believes that the potential for emotional experience resides in various subcortical regions of the brain. According to him, these neural substrates eventually develop into different emotional systems with the capacity for rage, fear, panic, sadness, play, joy, lust, and love. J. E. LeDoux (1996, 1999) emphasizes the role of the amygdala and its connections to subcortical and cortical neural networks in the regulation of fear reactions. A. N. Schore (1994, 1999) hypothesizes that the attachment experience of infants with their mothers is encoded in the right hemisphere and is critical for future emotional regulation. Initial emotional awareness occurs during a critical period of childhood development through a process termed *affective attunement* (Bion 1962, 1965; Stern 1985; Emde 1990), a complex interaction between the mother or caregiver and the child during which the mother intuits the child's feelings, then identifies and expresses them to the child, who in turn also learns to identify and communicate them. Sometimes, this process does not occur normally because the mother is emotionally impaired or unavailable. Under these circumstances, a child may grow into adulthood without the ability to identify and express feelings or to integrate language and feelings. This may result in a clinical condition known as alexithymia, characterized by the inability to identify, experience, and communicate feelings (Sifneos 1973; Nemiah 1977; Taylor, Bagby, and Parker 1997). Some children are exposed during childhood to severe physical or emotional trauma associated with intense physical or psychic pain. Their only means of self-protection is to suppress or deny the pain psychologically. This mode of self-defense may evolve into adult psychological defense mechanisms, including denial, suppression, and dissociation. Those individuals who employ these defense mechanisms are unable to experience a varied range and intensity of emotional life. On the other hand, there are individuals who, as a result of inborn temperament or faulty learning, experience overly intense and sometimes overwhelming feelings. Everyone needs to regulate or control feelings for the purpose of inner equilibrium and social appropriateness. This is normally accomplished using conscious and unconscious psychological defense mechanisms. For example, a conscious defense mechanism may be disavowal of an embarrassing statement or remark (denial). Examples of unconscious defense mechanisms are forgetting an unpleasant experience (repression) or blaming someone else for one's own mistake (projection). A variety of other defense mechanisms are used throughout waking life, including suppression, displacement, intellectualization, rationalization, sublimation, reaction formation, and undoing. Unpleasant or painful feelings are often neutralized by means of another defense mechanism known as isolation. In general, emotional regulation during waking life is accomplished by the conscious and unconscious activity of defense mechanisms.

DREAMING AND EMOTIONS

Dreaming is an inborn unconscious activity that involves regulating and controlling feelings (Kramer and Roth 1973; Kramer 1992, 1993; Kramer and Glucksman 2006). The mechanisms of the dreamwork (symbolism, displacement, condensation) may censor, modify, or enhance emotions. Occasionally, an emotion is so intense in a dream that it cannot be contained and is instead experienced to the point that it wakes the dreamer. In children, these dreams are referred to as *night terrors* and usually occur during non-REM sleep (Siegler 1987). In adults, they are termed *nightmares* and occur during REM sleep (Mack 1970; Hartmann 1984). Dream researchers have noted that mood on the day following a dream seems to be determined by the efficiency or inefficiency of the dreamwork to regulate feelings (Kramer and Roth 1980; Kramer and Brik 2002). For example, a man anticipated giving an important presentation at work and dreamed that he was in the jungle surrounded by a group of cannibals who were about to boil him alive. He was so terrified that he awoke feeling tense and anxious. He continued to experience these feelings the following day and was extremely apprehensive before and during his presentation. In this instance, the dreamer was unable to regulate his fear of attack in the dream and, subsequently, during his presentation the next day. On the other hand, a woman college professor was preparing to give a lecture to a group of visiting academics. The night before, she dreamed that she was conducting an orchestra and received a standing ovation after the performance. The next day, feeling relaxed and confident, she proceeded to give an excellent lecture that was well received. These are extreme examples of how dreams may or may not regulate feelings that affect the dreamer's conscious experience on the following day.

In each of the foregoing examples, the dreamer did nothing in a conscious way to influence the dream or its outcome. On the whole, the majority of people regulate their emotions automatically and unconsciously, particularly in their dreams. Most often, they are unaware of why they wake up in a particular mood, which may persist throughout the day. However, it is possible to monitor nightly dreams, paying particular attention to their affective component, in order to understand and change one's emotional state and behavior. For example, a woman was fearful of flying in airplanes but did not understand the source of her fear. One night, she dreamed that she was sitting on the nose of an airplane that was flying at a high altitude. Even though the wind was blowing strongly, she felt free and safe. However, she gradually became afraid of falling off the plane and went inside, where she once again felt secure. Her associations led to her fear of heights and falling. Moreover, she was afraid of being confined inside a plane without any control over the pilot's actions. It became clear that her fear of falling and not being in control were central factors contributing to her flying phobia. Once she became aware of these feelings and their irrational basis, she found it easier to overcome her phobia.

A man was extremely irritated with a fellow employee, who was uncooperative and shirked his responsibilities. Suppressing these feelings, he was consciously polite and civil to this other employee. One night, he dreamed that he shot him but didn't kill him because the bullets were blanks. When he realized the other man wasn't dead, he told him off in blunt language. This dream informed the dreamer that he was so angry with the other man that he felt like killing him but was restrained by his conscience. However, he was able to tell him how he felt about him in no uncertain terms. This enabled him to confront the other man about his annoying behavior in a more constructive way the following day.

Dreams often inform us of the underlying reasons for our conscious moods and feelings. A woman executive began experiencing tension and anxiety on a daily basis. She had repetitive dreams in which she found herself unprepared for an exam, unable to find the right classroom, and unable to remember where she lived. In the course of exploring these themes, she realized that she felt overwhelmed by the recent increase in the responsibilities of her job. She felt unprepared for her presentations at meetings and unable to meet deadlines for her reports. This awareness led her to delegate some of her projects, leading to a decrease in her anxiety.

A man involved in a romantic relationship continually doubted his girlfriend's love for him. Although her words and behavior indicated that she loved him very much, he remained unconvinced and distrustful of her love. One night, he dreamed that he witnessed a fatal helicopter crash. He felt frightened and sad in the dream. His associations led him to recall a former girlfriend who rejected him, then joined the air force. He later heard from a mutual friend that she had married a helicopter pilot. Prior to meeting his current girlfriend, he had been involved in a long-term relationship with another woman who had an affair with her boss while she was dating him. He felt betrayed and abandoned by both women, leading to his distrust of his present girlfriend. Recognizing the source of his feelings, he realized that he was confusing her with the other two women. This enabled him to perceive her more realistically and to commit himself more fully to the relationship.

A successful businessman constantly felt insecure and afraid of making the wrong decisions. He was particularly concerned about being judged as incompetent by his male peers. One night, he dreamed that he was participating in a quiz show with other male contestants. The questions pertained to his business, and he thought he answered them correctly. However, the judges (one of whom was his father) gave him a low score. He was devastated and felt like a failure. In reality, his father had been extremely critical and told him he would never amount to anything when he grew up. He realized that even though he was effective and successful at his work, he expected other men to judge him as his father did. This insight helped him to begin changing his self-image in accordance with his actual accomplishments.

A woman who was shy and self-conscious in social situations dreamed that she was in the cafeteria at work, eating lunch with a group of fellow employees. Everyone was engaged in active conversation except her. Each time she began to speak, her words came out in a confused manner. She felt embarrassed and stupid in front of her colleagues. The dream indicated that her social anxiety was connected to her fear of sounding confused and ignorant when she spoke with others. As a result, she always remained quiet in social situations in order to avoid embarrassing herself. Her awareness of the source of her verbal inhibitions led her to begin taking more risks in conversations at work and socially.

Another woman found herself feeling vaguely apprehensive and dreading the future. She dreamed that she was in a circle of people surrounded by large black snakes. Each person was given a snake and had no choice but to take it. She screamed out in terror, "I don't want the snake!" but was forced to hold it. Her associations included the recent deaths of several friends and family members. Moreover, she had been frightened by a mammogram taken just prior to the dream that revealed some questionable changes. However, they turned out to be normal. Nevertheless, she continued to feel apprehensive and preoccupied with the possibility of future breast cancer and death. The black snakes clearly symbolized her potential death and the deaths of others close to her. This dream helped her to understand the nature of her dread and facilitated an exploration of the meaning of her mortality. In doing so, her apprehension and uneasiness regarding the future began to diminish. In the foregoing examples, each of the dreamers was helped to understand why he or she was experiencing a particular mood or feeling on the basis of information provided by the dream. Often, the feelings were dramatically apparent in the dream; examples include the anxious woman executive who was unprepared for exams in her dreams, the man who felt devastated when he failed the quiz, or the woman who was terrified of holding the black snake.

Feelings may often be more symbolic than explicit in dreams. For example, a woman who was divorced complained of her former husband's immaturity and irresponsibility. She dreamed that she was swimming across a lake carrying her ex-husband on her back. His weight caused her great difficulty in swimming, and she wished she could get him "off her back." Indeed, carrying her husband on her back was exactly the way she felt during her marriage.

A man who was frequently annoyed with his boss because of the latter's constant criticism dreamed that he was in a museum, where he saw a painting that was predominantly red in color. His office was near a museum where he often went to "cool off" when he was irritated with his boss. The red color of the painting reminded him of the intensity of his anger. The foregoing examples illustrate how feelings are symbolized, rather than directly experienced in dreams.

Certain individuals are unable to experience their feelings while awake, either because they use defense mechanisms to keep their feelings from becoming conscious (e.g., denial, isolation, dissociation) or because they failed to learn how to identify and communicate their feelings during their formative years (alexithymia). The dreams of these individuals are characterized by the absence of feelings, amorphous feelings, or highly symbolized feelings. For example, a woman had repetitive dreams in which she was walking through a gray mist. She was raised in a family where feelings were never expressed, especially not unpleasant ones. Consequently, she experienced a chronic inner numbness and was unable to identify or describe any type of feeling. The gray mist in her dreams symbolized the amorphousness of her feelings.

A man reported only action and events in his dreams; that is, he was either engaged in athletic pursuits, driving his car, or fixing things. He had no conscious fantasy life and related to others in a concrete way, referring only to facts and events, never feelings. The total absence of feelings in his dream imagery reflected the emotional void in his waking life. On the other hand, dreams may also reflect overwhelming feelings and emotional chaos. For example, a woman dreamed that she was walking across a bridge when a tornado occurred. The bridge began swaying and then collapsed. She was thrown into the water and began to drown. This individual was extremely fragile emotionally. As a child, she was subjected to psychological and physical abuse. She lived in constant fear and was exquisitely sensitive to perceived slights and rejection from others. At the time of this dream, she felt isolated and excluded by others at work. The tornado represented her internal feelings of rage and despondency, which led to a suicide attempt shortly after she had this dream.

A woman with a history of bipolar disorder and manic episodes dreamed that she was on a swing when it took off and went sailing through the air. She felt totally out of control but excited at the same time. This dream occurred shortly before she began exhibiting symptoms of another manic episode.

The imagery in the two preceding dreams symbolically portrayed feelings that were out of the dreamer's control and later resulted in catastrophic behavior. Moreover, they functioned as early warning signals that informed the dreamer, as well as the therapist, that a major behavioral change was about to take place in the dreamer's life. In this sense, dreams can function as predictors of future behavior and provide information that can be used therapeutically, as well as preventatively. Whether symbolized or directly experienced in dreams, feelings can explain, amplify, or predict conscious behavior. They are often more graphically presented in dream imagery than consciously experienced (e.g., the black snake symbolizing death) and are frequently more exaggerated when experienced in dreams (e.g., terror of being boiled alive). Yet, their dramatic, sometimes distorted, presentation conveys an honesty and directness that facilitates an acute awareness of the issue at hand. The terror of being boiled alive certainly communicates the nature of the fright experienced by the man anticipating attack from a hostile audience. Similarly, being forced to hold a black snake against her will clearly reflects the degree of foreboding the dreamer felt in connection with her future death. In contrast, the absence of definitive feelings within oneself is accurately portrayed by the woman walking through the gray mist. The meaning and poignancy of these human experiences, as well as the emotions connected to them, would be blunted, if not entirely missed, were it not for the dream imagery. Therefore, when feelings are identified either through symbolism or direct experience in dream imagery, they can help the dreamer in a variety of ways. First, they can expose specific feelings that are only vaguely sensed consciously, or perhaps not at all. Following exposure and identification, they can help the dreamer clarify the issues, conflicts, or problems giving rise to the feelings. Following clarification, the dreamer can organize and initiate a constructive internal or external response. For example, the man who was terrified of being boiled alive could have recognized how terrified he was of the perceived hostility of his audience. This awareness might have enabled him to assess the degree of the reality of his perception. If he concluded that his assessment was incorrect, he could have modified his attitude toward the audience and felt less threatened during his presentation. On the other hand, if he had concluded that his assessment was correct, he could have altered his presentation and the manner in which he gave it so that the audience would not react with hostility. Likewise, the woman who was afraid to hold the snake in her dream became aware that the snake was synonymous with death. This enabled her to understand that her conscious feeling of foreboding was connected to her fear of the future deaths of herself and those close to her. As a result of this insight, she began talking about her fantasies concerning death and dying. The process of sharing her fantasies and feelings with an empathic therapist helped to diminish her sense of foreboding. The following vignettes illustrate how dreamers were able to identify, clarify, organize, and respond to feelings in their dreams.

A professional woman with two small children found herself growing increasingly irritated with her mother-in-law, who kept making excuses whenever she was asked to babysit. The woman complained to her husband about his mother's uncooperativeness, but he refused to intervene. One night, she dreamed that she was stabbing another woman and was enjoying it. Although she was horrified by her behavior in the dream, she realized that her anger toward her mother-in-law was reaching murderous proportions. Instead of complaining again to her husband, she arranged to have lunch with her mother-in-law. In the course of conversation, she told her how disappointed and hurt she felt over her unavailability to babysit. Her mother-in-law apologized and revealed how uneasy she felt about having the responsibility of taking care of two young children. The woman expressed confidence in her, and following this reassurance, her mother-in-law agreed to babysit. This vignette illustrates how an intense feeling can be identified (murderous rage), clarified (hurt and disappointment over lack of support, e.g., babysitting), and organized and responded to (inviting her mother-in-law to lunch and discussing the issue with her). These steps fortunately led to a constructive resolution.

A successful male executive was required to make frequent public presentations as part of his job. He always felt anxious and inhibited before he spoke and dreaded these occasions. One night, he dreamed that he was at a meeting where he was one of the featured speakers. Several colleagues spoke before he did, and he felt that each one was far superior to him. He awaited his turn feeling very anxious but was never called upon to speak. This dream highlighted a major source of his anxiety, namely, that others would invariably overshadow him, leading to public embarrassment. In the dream, he protected himself from embarrassment by not being asked to speak. After having this dream, he was able to identify and clarify the source of his anxiety connected to public speaking, that is, his fear of an inferior performance compared to other presenters. This insight led to an exploration of his anxiety in situations that he perceived as competitive. Invariably, his assumption was that he would either fail or perform poorly. This assumption was based on a lack of confidence in his own capabilities that was connected to childhood criticism by his father. Arrival at this insight led to a more realistic appraisal of his personality assets and abilities. Following this, he felt less anxiety and fear of embarrassment when speaking in public.

A recently widowed woman dreamed, "My mother and I were shopping for a new car for me. I chose a baby blue convertible, and my mother encouraged me to buy it. I was very excited and bought it, but it turned into a beat-up pickup truck. I was disappointed and told the salesman I wanted the convertible. It reappeared, but the paint was rusted, and I wondered what happened to it." Following the death of her husband, the dreamer withdrew socially and became quite reclusive. Her husband died of alcoholism; the latter problem had led to bitterness and disappointment in her marriage. Shortly before the dream, an old friend, who was a widower, had asked her out. She looked forward to seeing him but was afraid of being disappointed again if she entered into another relationship. Her mother had lived with her for many years after the dreamer's father died and never dated another man until her death. The dreamer's favorite color was blue, and the convertible represented freedom, happiness, and sexual pleasure for her. The rusted truck and car meant deterioration, ageing, and unhappiness. The dream portrayed her conflict about whether to start another phase of her life and pursue the promise of a new relationship and potential happiness or to continue with her social withdrawal and live a lonely, unhappy life as her mother did. After discussing the implications of the dream with her therapist, she chose to go out with her friend and began socializing again.

A young musician was invited to play with a band that was becoming quite popular. Although his talent was widely acknowledged by others, he felt insecure and harbored doubts about his ability to perform effectively with the band. He dreamed, "I was asked to be a keyboardist for a band called Phish. We performed at the White House, and the band then got on the presidential helicopter. It took off without me; however, I managed to hang on to it and finally climbed aboard. It seemed easy, and I was having fun." This dream reflected his ambivalence about playing in the band. On the one hand, he wanted to be successful and honored (playing for the president). On the other hand, he was afraid of being rejected and excluded (missing the band's helicopter). He associated Phish to a well-known contemporary band, as well as to pleasurable fishing trips with his father, who was also a musician and very supportive of his career. In reality, he was a keyboardist for whom performing was easy and fulfilling when he felt secure with his playing. After recognizing his ambivalent feelings, as well as the joy and ease he felt when he actually performed, he accepted the offer to join the band.

The foregoing examples illustrate how the emotional component of dreams can be used to identify feelings, understand waking moods, and effectively organize conscious behavior on the basis of information provided by feelings that are experienced or symbolized in dreams.

The following steps can be taken by therapists and clients for the purpose of analyzing and constructively utilizing feelings in dreams:

1. Identify and elaborate on the feelings and emotions experienced in the dream. Connect the feelings to relevant current or past experiences evoked by the manifest imagery.
2. Identify images and symbols (e.g., colors, objects, movements, facial expressions) in the manifest content that suggest or symbolize feelings.
3. Identify the client's mood upon awakening. Is it connected to the imagery and feelings experienced or symbolized in the previous night's dreams?
4. Connect the feelings and mood associated with the dream to significant current or past relationships and to the self-image of the client.
5. Assess whether or not there is a realistic or unrealistic basis for the feelings experienced or symbolized in the dream. If realistic, attempt to have the client honestly acknowledge and accept them. If unrealistic, explore with the client the reason(s) for them and attempt to resolve the conflict(s) or issue(s) involved.
6. If necessary, attempt to modify the client's current or future expectations, beliefs, or actions connected to the feelings or mood in the dream.
7. Use the dream as a point of reference when similar feelings or moods occur in the future.

REFERENCES

Bion, W. R. 1962. *Learning from experience*. London: Heinemann.
———. 1965. *Transformation*. London: Heinemann.
Emde, R. N. 1990. Mobilizing fundamental modes of development: Empathic availability and therapeutic action. *J. of the American Psychoanalytic Association* 38:881–913.
Hartmann, E. 1984. *The nightmare: The psychology and biology of terrifying dreams*. New York: Basic Books.
Kramer, M. 1992. Mood change from night to morning. *Sleep Research* 21:153.
———. 1993. The selective mood regulatory function of dreaming: An update and revision. In *The functions of dreaming*, ed. A. Moffitt, M. Kramer, and R. Hoffmann, 139–95. Albany: State University of New York Press.
Kramer, M., and I. Brik. 2002. Affective processing by dreams across the night. *Sleep* 25 (Supplement): A180–81.

Kramer, M., and M. L. Glucksman. 2006. Changes in manifest dream affect during psychoanalytic treatment. *J. of the American Academy of Psychoanalysis and Dynamic Psychiatry* 34, no. 2:249–60.

Kramer, M., and T. Roth. 1973. The mood-regulating function of sleep. In *Sleep: Physiology, biochemistry, psychology, pharmacology, clinical implications*, ed. W. P. Koella and P. Levin, 563–71. First European Congress on Sleep Research. Basel, Switzerland: S. Karger.

———. 1980. The relationship of dream content to night-morning mood change. In *Sleep 1978*, ed. L. Popoviciu, B. Asgian, G. Badin, 621–24. Fourth European Congress on Sleep Research, Tigre-Migres. Basel, Switzerland: S. Karger.

LeDoux, J. E. 1996. *The emotional brain: The mysterious underpinnings of emotional life*. New York: Simon and Schuster.

———. 1999. Commentary: Psychoanalytic theory: Clues from the brain. *Neuro-Psychoanalysis* 1, no. 1:44–49.

Mack, J. E. 1970. *Nightmares and human conflict*. Boston: Little, Brown and Co.

Nemiah, J. C. 1977. Alexithymia: Theoretical considerations. *Psychotherapy and Psychosomatics* 28:199–206.

Panksepp, J. 1998. *Affective neuroscience: The foundation of human and animal emotions*. New York: Oxford University Press.

———. 1999. Emotions as viewed by psychoanalysis and neuroscience: An exercise in consilience. *Neuro-Psychoanalysis* 1, no. 1:15–38.

———. 2001. The long-term psychobiological consequences of infant emotions: Prescriptions for the twenty-first century. *Neuro-Psychoanalysis* 3, no. 2:149–78.

Schore, A. N. 1994. *Affect regulation and the origin of the self: The neurobiology of emotional development*. Hillsdale, NJ: Lawrence Erlbaum.

———. 1999. Commentary on: Emotions as viewed by psychoanalysis and neuroscience: an exercise in consilience (by J. Panksepp). *Neuro-Psychoanalysis* 1, no. 1: 49–55.

Siegler, A. L. 1987. The nightmare and child development: Some observations from a psychoanalytic perspective. In *The nightmare: psychological and biological foundations*, ed. H. Kellerman, 198–214. New York: Columbia University Press.

Sifneos, P. E. 1973. The prevalence of 'alexithymic' characteristics in psychosomatic patients. *Psychotherapy and Psychosomatics* 22:255–62.

Stern, D. N. 1985. *The interpersonal world of the infant*. New York: Basic Books.

Taylor, G. J., R. M. Bagby, and J. D. A. Parker. 1997. *Disorders of affect regulation: alexithymia in medical and psychiatric disorders*. Cambridge: Cambridge University Press.

SUGGESTED READING

Demascio, A. 1994. *Descartes' error: Emotion, reason, and the human brain*. New York: G. P. Putnam.

———. 1999. *The feeling of what happens: Body and emotion in the making of consciousness*. New York: Harcourt, Brace.

Emde, R. 1990. Toward a psychoanalytic theory of affect: I. The organizational model and its propositions. In *The course of life: Infancy*, ed. S. Greenspan and G. Pollock, 165–91. 2nd ed. New York: International Universities Press.

Freud, S. 1915[1957]. Instincts and their vicissitudes. In *The standard edition of the complete psychological works of Sigmund Freud*, ed. and trans. J. Strachey, Vol. 14, 109–40. London: Hogarth Press.

Izard, C. E. 1977. *Human emotions*. New York: Plenum Press.

Levin, F. M. 1991. *Mapping the mind*. Hillsdale, NJ: The Analytic Press.

Panksepp, J. 1998. *Affective neuroscience*. New York: Oxford University Press.

Reiser, M. F. 1984. *Mind, brain, body: Toward a convergence of psychoanalysis and neurobiology*. New York: Basic Books.

4

Relationships with Others

DEVELOPMENT OF RELATIONSHIPS

Even though dreams are created within the self, they often reflect our perceptions, attitudes, and interactions with others. We live in the context of our relationships within marriage, friendship, work, family, community, and society. Relationships can be both pleasurable and satisfying, or they can be threatening and unpleasant. Our deepest wishes, hopes, fears, humiliations, and fulfillments occur within relationships. Personality development is heavily influenced by the child's relationships with others, namely parents and caregivers. An interior mental landscape of interactions with mother and important others gradually develops during infancy and childhood. This inner world of relationships is termed *internal object relations* (Fairbairn 1952; Kernberg 1976; Greenberg and Mitchell 1983). The child's perceptions of others and relationships with them are internalized in conjunction with the emotions associated with them. These internalized object relations are further modified, and sometimes distorted, by the child's subjective needs (Ogden, 1990; Grotstein 2000). Internal objects are frequently transformed into images, symbols, and fantasies. In turn, these internal objects may be incorporated into the manifest content of dreams. As a result, dreams frequently reflect our idiosyncratic perceptions of the external world, as well as the vicissitudes of our interpersonal relationships and the feelings generated by them. Relationships in dreams can be either gratifying and pleasurable or conflicted and painful. Sometimes, dreams reflect the status of a current relationship. Often, they examine the problems or conflicts in that relationship. In doing so, they may reflect our emotional reactions to the other person, as well as our attempts to improve or repair the relationship. Frequently, the person(s) in the dream may be a displacement of the individual(s) about whom the dreamer is concerned. Such displacements may include people from the past or present who resonate with the individual(s) in the current relationship that is under consideration. Displacements may also occur in the form of animals or inanimate objects, such as clothing, places, or words.

CATEGORIES OF RELATIONSHIPS

In order to understand how relationships are portrayed in dreams, we can arbitrarily categorize them. For example, some dreams deal with rejection or abandonment by others. Another frequent theme is competition and rivalry. Feelings of hurt and sadness usually accompany the former, while envy and jealousy are associated with the latter. Another common theme is love and acceptance by others. Affirmation, support, and recognition are related themes. Happiness, joy, and well-being are some of the feelings connected to these dreams. Romantic dreams often include emotional and sexual intimacy. However, sex and passion may occur in them without emotional closeness. By the same token, friendship and emotional intimacy in dreams are not always accompanied by sexual feelings or activity. Sometimes, sexual activity is symbolic of emotional closeness and cannot be taken only literally. Likewise, sexual relationships in dream content may reflect other issues, including dominance, submission, dependency, sadism, and masochism. Ambivalence toward others is frequently encountered in dream content. Issues of affection, hate, trust, control, power, dependency, and autonomy are often involved in these dreams. Specific types of relationships may be focused on, including marital, parental, and sibling relationships; friendships; and employer-employee relationships. Love, hate, affection, disinterest, caring, trust, fear, cooperation, suspicion, betrayal, and security are part of the spectrum of feelings found in dreams dealing with specific relationships. In addition to feelings, other elements make up the fabric of dreams about relationships, including self-image, self-identity, conflicts, problems, and decision making.

The following are examples of dreams that fall into the various categories of interpersonal relationships.

Rejection and Abandonment

A woman suffering from a chronic illness felt that no one appreciated the severity of her symptoms. She had the following dream: "I was very sick and needed help. My husband and doctors were at my bedside, but they seemed oblivious to me and offered no help." She felt that her husband was emotionally insensitive and reacted toward her as though she were in normal health. Moreover, she was very critical of her doctors because they were unable to relieve her of her pain. Historically, she experienced her parents as unloving and inattentive to her needs. Analyzing the dream helped her to make a connection between her parents' rejection and the way she perceived the behavior of her husband and doctors.

A woman's mother was very ill and living in another city. She dreamed the following: "My mother and grandmother were in rocking chairs with their faces turned away from me. I called to them, but they didn't hear me. I was scared." The dreamer was afraid that her mother was going to die, as her grandmother and father had earlier. She had ambivalent feelings toward her mother and wanted to resolve them before her mother's death. The anticipation of her mother's death left her feeling abandoned and alone. The dream paved the way for her to visit her mother and work through her ambivalent feelings toward her.

A woman who was married for the second time was insecure about her husband's fidelity. She dreamed, "My husband was in love with a younger woman. She had red hair. He wanted to leave me, and I begged him not to. He was oblivious to me." Her former husband was remarried to a woman with red hair. Furthermore, her mother had left her father when she was six and never returned. Her father remarried and sent her off to boarding school. Her present husband was emotionally remote and could only show his affection through sex. She was exquisitely sensitive to rejection and abandonment as a consequence of her past history. This dream enabled her to understand the origin of her expectation of rejection and betrayal by her husband.

A male executive accidentally discovered that a friend of his who worked for another company was looking for someone to fill a job opening. It was a desirable position, and he was dismayed that his friend had not told him about it. He dreamed, "I was in a car and Mike was the driver. He was driving recklessly, and the passenger side door suddenly opened, throwing me out onto the road. Miraculously, I was not hurt, but I pretended to be so that he would feel guilty." The dreamer felt hurt and rejected when his friend (Mike) failed to tell him about the job opening. He associated the reckless driving to his friend's insensitivity in their relationship. His first impulse was to call his friend and tell him how hurt and annoyed he was in order to make him feel guilty. After reflecting on the dream, he decided to call his friend and mention that he had heard about the job opening but not disclose his real feelings. His friend responded by telling him that, indeed, he had thought of him for the job, but the position had been cancelled. The dreamer felt relieved that he had withheld expressing his initial feelings.

Loss and Separation

The only brother of a divorced woman died rather suddenly. She dreamed the following: "I was standing on a pier holding my former husband in my arms. He was dead. There had been a nuclear holocaust, and other dead bodies floated in the water." She had been extremely close to her brother and felt bereft when he died. Her former husband had left her shortly after her mother died. She was devastated at that time and felt like her world had blown up. She felt similarly when her brother died. This dream confronted her with the depth of her depressive state, motivating her to seek treatment.

A married woman with two young sons had a potentially fatal illness. She dreamed, "I was picking up my sons from camp, but I couldn't find them. I kept yelling out for them. Then, I realized that someone had taken them. I cried." The dreamer was afraid that she would die prematurely from her illness and leave her sons without a mother. She was concerned about their loss of a mother and her separation from them when she died. Following this dream, she confided in her husband, who reassured her that he would devote himself to raising their sons if she were to die.

A married man felt that his wife was emotionally remote and sexually rejecting. He dreamed, "My wife and I had split up; however, we were trying to meet again. I got on a bus to meet her, but it went in the wrong direction. I was worried that we wouldn't hook up again." The dreamer was pessimistic about the possibility of a change in his wife's behavior and anticipated the loss of his marriage. The dream spurred him to seek couple counseling.

Competition and Rivalry

A successful businessman dreamed the following: "I was in a contest with another man. It had to do with who could make a better verbal presentation about food and beverage topics. The other man was a banker, and I was sure that I would win. But the judges weren't impressed with me; they thought I was unpolished and unprofessional. I was given a lower score than the other contestant and felt very upset and humiliated. I realized that my father, family, and friends would know that I failed an important test of my accomplishments." The dreamer was a successful food distributor but was constantly afraid of being criticized and of failing. His father was demeaning and punitive while he was growing up and told him he would never amount to anything. Although he had been recently appointed to serve on the board of trustees of a large company, he felt inferior to the other trustees. The insight provided by this dream helped him to address his fears of criticism and failure.

A married woman was extremely possessive and jealous of her husband's relationships with other women. Her father had always favored her sister, whom she envied. She dreamed, "I was with my friend Anne and my husband. She was dressed in a yellow outfit and looked great. I knew he was attracted to her, and I felt fat and ugly compared to her." The dreamer was actually quite attractive; while growing up, her father repeatedly said that she was smart but her sister was prettier. As a consequence, her relationships with other women were marked by distrust, feelings of inferiority about her physical appearance, and competitiveness. This dream helped her to understand how her sibling rivalry, augmented by her father, led to her problematic relationships with other women.

A very successful man was always comparing himself unfavorably with other men. He was constantly afraid that others would discover his weak points and expose him. He had the following dream: "I was riding my bike with Bob, and we were going up a very steep hill. Bob fell off his bike, and I felt good about it. I felt superior and gloated over his misfortune." Although Bob was one of his closest friends, he nevertheless felt inferior to him. In order to build up his self-esteem, he often looked for Bob's vulnerabilities and sometimes made sarcastic remarks about them. He did this with other friends as well. His father was emotionally remote and never complimented him. As a result, he always felt like a failure in his father's eyes. This insight enabled him to understand why he demeaned other men.

Fear of Emotional or Physical Injury

A woman executive had just started a new job. She was afraid of not succeeding and had heard that her predecessor was fired. She dreamed, "I was at home and saw a forest fire coming toward my house. I ran into the cellar. Trees were falling, and the house caught fire. I was terrified." She was afraid of failing at her job and suffering the same fate as her predecessor; in other words, she feared that she would also be "fired." She recalled that her father lost his job when she was very young and how frightened she was at the time. After she made this connection, she felt less anxious about being fired.

An adolescent boy had recently transferred to a new school. He dreamed, "I was at school in biology class. I didn't know any of the kids, and the teacher was yelling at us. One of the kids started beating up the teacher. But the teacher beat up the kid and began punching other kids, including me. I escaped through the window and told my mother." The dreamer's father was a large man who frequently lost his temper and yelled loudly at his son. The dreamer also had an older brother who bullied him and occasionally beat him up. He sought protection from his mother, but she was not always available.

Transferring to the new school heightened his fears of physical injury and psychological harassment. A trusting, supportive relationship with his male therapist helped to allay his anxiety, and he was able to attend school.

A single woman with a female roommate was in a new relationship with a man. One evening, he telephoned, and her roommate answered. The roommate had a prolonged conversation with him that aroused the woman's jealousy. That night, she dreamed, "I was hiking on a trail with my sister. Suddenly, she yelled out, 'There's a snake, and I need your help!' It was gigantic, with horns, and I took a whack at it with a stick. It lunged at me and bit me. I felt a horrible pain." Her sister represented her roommate, and the snake symbolized her roommate's betrayal of her by attempting to gain her boyfriend's attention. As a child, she felt that she was her father's favorite until he began paying more attention to her sister. She recalled this as a painful betrayal that sensitized her to potential betrayals in the future. This insight helped her to feel less jealous of her roommate.

A man in a business partnership felt that his partners were taking advantage of him and could not be trusted. He dreamed, "I was on an island and was being held prisoner by some crooks. I was afraid they were going to kill me, and there was no way to escape." The dream portrayed his feeling of being trapped in the partnership and vulnerable to his partners. He recalled that his father was controlling and punitive, which made him feel vulnerable and helpless. He grew up believing that other men would harm him in some fashion and that he was helpless to protect himself. The realization that his sense of vulnerability with other men was connected to his relationship with his father helped him to understand an important source of his distrust of his partners.

Affirmation and Recognition

A woman writer was having difficulty completing a novel. She had enjoyed some success with previous works but was apprehensive about the public's reaction to her current project. She dreamed, "I was in a performing troupe. Frank Sinatra appeared and asked me how I was doing. I told him I was working on a book, but it wasn't progressing well. He suggested that I go on tour with him as a performer. I felt good." She associated Frank Sinatra to a successful male novelist whom she knew. His favorite singer happened to be Frank Sinatra. In addition, he was very supportive and encouraging of her work. Her wish was to be as successful as her novelist friend was and to go on book tours as he did. Following this dream, she felt increased self-confidence and a renewed energy for writing.

A male college professor was concerned about receiving tenure. He dreamed, "I was talking with Dr. T., and he told me that I was going to receive an academic award. I felt pleased and recognized." Dr. T. was the chairman of the dreamer's department and would be instrumental in recommending him for tenure. His recent work had drawn favorable attention, and he hoped that Dr. T. knew about it so that he would recommend him for tenure.

A female executive worked in an all-male department. She felt that there was a glass ceiling in her company and that she would have difficulty obtaining a promotion. She dreamed, "I was giving a presentation to a group of men. John and Mike were there, along with some other men from my department. They were nodding approval, and I felt recognized for my professional capabilities." John and Mike were coworkers involved in a joint project with her. She felt that they liked her and respected her abilities. Her hope was that, with their support, she would receive a promotion.

Affection, Love, and Intimacy

A married woman entered therapy because of an unhappy, loveless marriage. After some time in treatment, she had the following dream: "I was dancing with a man who was leading me with my left hand. We were gliding along, and I had a pleasant, nice, loving feeling." She associated the man to her male therapist, whom she felt understood her and was very caring. At the time of the dream, she was fantasizing about having an affair with him. The fact that he was leading her by the left (wrong) hand meant that it would be inappropriate for her to pursue an actual romantic relationship with him.

A man with a long history of feeling emotionally isolated from others was in group therapy for several years. He reported the following dream after a group session: "I was in group therapy and found myself lying naked with Helen. I told her I admired and respected her. I felt a new-found intimacy with her and reveled in it." Helen was a woman in the group whom he felt was his severest critic. However, in the group session prior to the dream, he had spoken honestly about his feelings, and Helen had complimented him for it. He sensed an emotional closeness with her that he had never felt for anyone before. Finding himself naked with her reflected his growing capacity to expose himself emotionally to her and the others in the group.

A man who constantly feared criticism from others and humiliation at his job was about to have a performance evaluation by his boss. He dreamed, "I met Bill at a restaurant. After we ate, he hugged me, and I felt a real sense of affection from him." Bill was his boss and was going to evaluate him. He hoped that Bill would give him a good evaluation. As a child, he felt fat and awkward, often finding himself the object of ridicule. His father was critical and unaffectionate, and he expected other men to behave similarly toward him. On the other hand, Bill had always been respectful and supportive. The dream enabled him to differentiate Bill from his father and to feel optimistic about Bill's evaluation of him.

Cooperativeness and Mutual Regard

A professional man with a long history of competitiveness and mistrust of others had the following dream after some years in therapy: "I was playing on a basketball team in a very intense game. I was surprised to find myself passing the ball to my teammates and having them pass it back to me. I scored some baskets and felt good about being a member of the team." At this point in his treatment, he felt more trusting of others and less competitive. He was more open and generous with his friends, and they, in turn, were friendlier toward him.

A married woman without children felt that she and her husband lived in social isolation. Both were busy professionals and immersed themselves in their work. She had been sent away to boarding school after her parents divorced and never felt a sense of belonging to a family. She dreamed, "My husband and I were out hiking. I asked him if we could build a cabin. He was reluctant until some friends came by. They agreed to help us, and we all built one together." The dream made her realize that she and her husband needed to reach out to others in order to end their social isolation. Building a cabin with friends symbolized this need to create a social community that would serve as an emotional home and family for them.

Dreams that are primarily concerned with interpersonal interactions can provide us with valuable insights about the nature of our relationships. They can be used to identify the nature or quality of our relationships and to help us assess what we need to change within ourselves in order to improve or modify them. They can also be used as a measure of how our relationships are actually changing; consider, for example, the man who became less competitive and dreamed that he was a contributing member of a team. Feelings and perceptions are important components of dreams about relationships. Sometimes, a troubled relationship remains unresolved in a dream, and the dreamer continues to experience unpleasant or painful feelings. At other times, a change takes place in the relationship, and the dreamer's mood improves. Prejudices, distortions, and misconceptions toward others are often reflected in dream imagery. This provides an opportunity for the dreamer to correct erroneous attitudes and to change inappropriate behavior in relationships. People who appear in a dream are not always who they seem to be, and the mechanism of displacement commonly occurs, whereby one individual may actually represent another. This occurred in the dream where Frank Sinatra appeared and was a displacement for a friend of the dreamer's. It is also important to keep in mind that even though the dreamer may not be personally involved in a dream, the people and their interactions may still have meaning and relevance. Whether they are bizarre, exaggerated, or realistic, dreams involving relationships can be extremely informative and helpful in enabling the dreamer to reassess and improve interactions with others.

In order to understand and use a dream that is primarily concerned with relationships, the following steps can be helpful for both the therapist and client:

1. Identify the major theme in the interpersonal encounter; is it positive, negative, or ambivalent?
2. Does the interaction between individuals fall into one or more of the categories previously defined? For example, is it about loss and separation? Is it about love and intimacy?
3. After identifying the major theme and category, have the client associate to past or present events, issues, and relationships that resonate with it.
4. Ask the client to reflect about individuals involved in those events or to evaluate relationships that the characters in the dream may represent.
5. Examine the client's relationship with those individuals and determine whether one of the characters in the dream is a displacement of the client or of someone else.
6. Ask the client whether he or she would like the relationship to be, or to have been, different. If so, explore with the client ways to change, or to have changed, it.
7. Determine whether the relationship is part of a familiar pattern, similar to significant relationships the client has had in the past with family members or others.
8. If there is evidence of a familiar pattern in the client's relationships, is it reflected in the client's relationship with the therapist? If so, explore the client-therapist relationship at an appropriate time.

REFERENCES

Fairbairn, W. R. D. 1952. *An object relations theory of personality.* New York: Basic Books.

Greenberg, J. R., and S. A. Mitchell. 1983. *Object relations in psychoanalytic theory.* Cambridge, MA: Harvard University Press.

Grotstein, J. S. 2000. *Who is the dreamer who dreams the dream?* Hillsdale, NJ: The Analytic Press.

Kernberg, O. 1976. *Object relations theory and clinical psychoanalysis*. New York: Jason Aronson.

Ogden, T. H. 1990. *The matrix of the mind*. New York: Jason Aronson.

Winnicott, D. W. 1953. Transitional objects and transitional phenomena. *International J. of Psychoanalysis* 34:89–97.

SUGGESTED READING

Guntrip, H. 1969. *Schizoid phenomena, object relations and the self*. New York: International Universities Press.

Levenson, E. 1985. The interpersonal model. In *Models of the mind*, ed. A. Rothstein, 57–59. New York: International Universities Press.

Schafer, R. 1968. *Aspects of internalization*. Madison, CT: International Universities Press.

Spitz, R. 1965. *The first year of life: A psychoanalytic study of normal and deviant development of object relations*. New York: International Universities Press.

Stolorow, R. D., B. Brandchaft, and G. E. Atwood. 1987. *Psychoanalytic treatment: An intersubjective approach*. Hillsdale, NJ: Analytic Press.

Sullivan, H. S. 1953. *The interpersonal theory of psychiatry*. New York: W. W. Norton.

Winnicott, D. W. 1989. *Psychoanalytic explorations*, ed. C. Winnicott, R. Shepherd, and M. Davis. Cambridge, MA: Harvard University Press.

5

Self-Identity

Since dreams are self-created, it follows that their content is often concerned with the self. Indeed, dreams are perhaps the most honest self-monitoring device we possess. The dreamer may appear undisguised, as an observer, or displaced by another person in the manifest content. In the same way that dreams portray our relationships with others, they also convey our sense of ourselves. In doing so, they offer us an opportunity to change various aspects of ourselves, including our self-image, personality characteristics, attitudes, beliefs, and behaviors.

DEVELOPMENT OF SELF

The self begins to develop at birth. However, until the age of two months, there is no discrete sense of a self. Feelings are also largely undifferentiated, consisting of precursor states of contentment and distress (Hesse and Cicchetti 1982). From two to nine months, the infant gradually develops an "emergent sense of self" (Stern 1985). During this time span, the attachment process facilitates a sense of security, as well as a tolerance for separation from the mother (Bowlby 1969, 1973). Between the seventh and ninth months of life, infants develop a sense of self that is separate from the mother (Stern 1985). Simultaneously, they are able to share subjective mental states with others, including attentional focus, intentional communication, and emotions. During the second year of life, children develop the ability to speak and to communicate with others through language. At the same time, they begin to see themselves objectively and to use their imagination (Piaget 1954; Stern

1985). As they continue to grow, this nascent sense of self is influenced by a variety of factors: their interactions with others, especially their caregivers; their physical development and increasing capacity for autonomy; their ability to remember their interactions with others and the behavior of others toward them; their capacity to differentiate, identify, and express feelings; their development of language skills and the ability to communicate their thoughts and feelings about themselves with others; their capacity to empathize with the mental states and behaviors of others. All of these factors combine to shape the development of a self-identity or self-representation. However, this self-identity is extremely plastic and can change within the context of interpersonal or environmental circumstances. As a result, the child's view of self is largely dependent on the attitudes and behavior of those around it. For example, a child may feel loveable and secure with a caring, supportive caregiver but vulnerable and insecure with an abusive, rejecting one. Gradually, a "core self-identity" develops over time, but it is nevertheless influenced and modified by the child's interpersonal, social context. Adolescence is a particularly volatile phase of self-development. It is a period marked by the confluence of multiple factors: the need to be accepted by peers; the development of sexual physical characteristics and sexual feelings; the need to be more autonomous from parental control; identification with role models, such as teachers, public figures, and celebrities. As a result, self-identity during adolescence is highly variable and unpredictable. Nevertheless, by early adulthood, a relatively stable core self-identity is established, including body image (perception of size, appearance, athletic ability, etc.), intellectual capacity (knowledge, ability to learn and problem solve, etc.), belief systems (values, morals), emotional resources (capacity to identify and appropriately express feelings), interpersonal abilities (capacity to form friendships and behave appropriately in different social contexts), and healthy narcissism (a positive sense of one's likeability, competence, social acceptability, etc). Of course, all of these elements that make up self-identity are changeable and influenced by culture, society, religion, and education. Moreover, self-identity remains malleable and is continuously influenced by life's experiences, feedback from others, successes, failures, health, illness, and social, political, and economic factors.

CATEGORIES OF DREAMS ABOUT THE SELF

Dreams provide a steady stream of information about self-identity at any given moment in our lives. Although we tend to protect our conscious sense of self-esteem and security by means of defense mechanisms, dreams are often less self-protective and may be more candid in their portrayals of self.

Sometimes, they exaggerate certain aspects of the self, as if to make a particular point. Like our feelings and relationships with others, they can be arbitrarily categorized according to their quality and content. For example, certain dreams deal with our sense of vulnerability, insecurity, and ineffectiveness. Other dreams are concerned with how we experience ourselves with others (as accepted, rejected, superior, inferior). Some dreams portray our personality characteristics (aggressive, passive, independent, dependent, suspicious, trustful). Many dreams reflect our physical or bodily experiences (attractive, ugly, fat, thin, sick, healthy). Sometimes, physiologic needs or sensations are expressed in dreams (hunger, sexual urges, physical pain). Self-identity and feelings are intimately connected and experienced in our dreams, including confidence, loss of control, helplessness, satisfaction, guilt, shame, anger, fear, sadness, joy, elation, and so on. Although every dream is a creation of the self and therefore a part of the self, certain dreams are especially concerned with aspects of self-experience. Some of these dreams are exclusively about the self ("self-state dreams"), while others contain imagery particularly relevant to the self. The following examples illustrate how dreams that primarily involve the self can be arbitrarily categorized and understood for the purpose of promoting change within the self.

Failure, Ineffectiveness

A married woman with young children developed a serious illness. Her medical treatment resulted in complications that impaired her daily functioning. She dreamed, "I was in a basketball game with other women. They were playing well, but the ball was very tiny, and I couldn't do anything with it. I felt frustrated and embarrassed." Her inability to handle the ball symbolized her feelings of ineffectiveness and her sense of failure in caring for her children. The other women in the game represented mothers whom she felt were more effective and competent in caring for their children. This realization motivated her to develop a more positive attitude toward coping with her illness. In turn, she became more self-confident as a mother.

A professional man with an excellent reputation took pride in being the best in his field. He dreamed, "I was playing golf with some other men. It was my turn to hit the ball, but I couldn't decide how to hit it. I finally took a swing, but I missed. I was embarrassed and walked away." His biggest fear was failing in front of others. Sometimes, he would avoid a project altogether if he felt there was a chance of failure. His father was always extremely critical whenever he made a mistake and humiliated him when he did. As a result, he became a perfectionist and avoided any possibility of failing. This insight enabled him to become less self-critical and to take more risks.

Vulnerability, Exposure

A woman always felt that she could never live up to others' expectations of her. She dreamed, "I was in the bathroom and heard a knock on the door. It was the mailman with a package, and he wanted to come in and give it to me. I felt naked and vulnerable." The bathroom reminded her of the one in the house where she grew up. Her belief that she could never please others stemmed from her parents' frequent criticism of her. As a consequence, she always felt in imminent danger of being exposed as inadequate. The dream helped her to understand the source of her feelings of inadequacy, and she began viewing herself with greater acceptance.

A woman with a childhood history of physical and verbal abuse entered treatment because of multiple incapacitating phobias. She dreamed, "A man's face was looking at me through a window. I was terrified that he was going to kill me. I tried to shout a warning to my sister and heard her shout, 'He's trying to kill us.' I was frantic and felt exposed and helpless." As a child, she and her sister were physically and verbally abused by their father. There were instances when she thought he would kill them. As a result, she grew up feeling frightened, vulnerable, and helpless. The dream enabled her to understand the origin of her phobias and to begin overcoming them.

A male executive felt insecure in his position at work and unable to commit himself to his girlfriend. He dreamed, "I was at a zoo and saw a giant animal that looked like a giraffe with horns. I knew that hunters were going to take its horns, but it looked at me and seemed unconcerned. I knew that I did not have the power to stop them or to save it. I felt powerless and ashamed of myself." The dreamer's company was reorganizing, and he was afraid that his job would be terminated. His boss had recently been let go, and he felt powerless to protect himself. He was tall in stature and identified with the giraffe. His relationship with his girlfriend was characterized by ambivalence and sexual impotence. He associated the giraffe's horns to male potency, and his lack of it in his relationship and at his job. Surgery for an undescended testis at age ten reinforced his fears of injury and castration as a boy. Further associations led to his childhood fear of his father's anger at him for his overly close relationship with his mother. As a result, his self-identity was shaped by feelings of vulnerability and powerlessness.

Rejection, Abandonment

A married woman was extremely jealous of her husband's relationships with other women. She dreamed, "I was with my parents and Bill at a party. We were all singing together. Bill started talking to Jean, and they went into another room. I tried to interrupt them, but Bill ordered me to go away." The dreamer's family was musical, but her father always said that her sister was more musically talented than she. This led to her constantly comparing herself to other women regarding her talents, appearance, and other qualities. She often felt rejected, especially in social situations, whenever she felt other women drew more attention than she. In particular, she was always vigilant of her husband's attention to other women. The dream provided her with further insight into how her insecurity with other women stemmed from her father's partiality toward her sister.

A married woman was receiving medical treatment for a serious illness. She dreamed, "I was very sick and in the hospital. All my doctors were gathered around me, but they didn't seem to know what to do. None of them were trying to help me, either." In reality, her doctors were very attentive to her. However, her expectation was that they, as well as others, would not be interested in her. She felt that her parents were never genuinely loving or emotionally involved with her. In addition, her husband was preoccupied with his work and not as attentive as she wanted him to be. As a result, she saw herself as emotionally abandoned and alone. The dream helped her understand how her experience of emotional rejection by her parents colored her perception of the behavior of others toward her.

Self-Image, Body Image

A successful woman executive found herself having frequent arguments with her peers and supervisors. She dreamed, "I saw a pig with two heads. One resembled a wild boar with a vicious look. The other was a baby with a soft, innocent face. I was struck by the difference between them." She associated to the opposite parts of herself; on the one hand, she could be greedy, confrontational, and vicious; on the other hand, she could be accommodating, generous, and kind. She realized that she needed to change the "wild boar" aspect of her personality in order to get along more harmoniously with others.

A male professional had difficulty with intimacy and forming friendships. The first dream he reported in therapy was the following: "I was about to have an operation for a brain tumor. I felt numb, in some kind of stupor." He associated the brain tumor to his difficulty in connecting emotionally with others. The numbness and stupor reflected his emotional inhibitions in his relationships. The operation he was undergoing represented the therapy he had just begun in order to correct the problem. His associations led to the lack of emotional communication between his parents and himself as he was growing up. As a consequence, he had difficulty experiencing and expressing his feelings.

The dream enabled him to understand an important source of his difficulty in establishing emotional intimacy with others.

An older woman who was nearing the end of her professional career dreamed, "I was with a group of young teachers. They asked me what I had accomplished in my career. I couldn't answer. I felt inadequate, fat, and old. Then I saw an old woman sitting on some steps. She couldn't walk or speak, and I felt sorry for her." The dream reflected how she felt about herself mentally and physically: aging, inadequate professionally, and overweight. The old woman was herself, in a state of psychological and physical deterioration. The dream not only helped her to understand why she felt so depressed but also motivated her to think about her past accomplishments and to consider what she was still capable of contributing as a professional.

Behavioral Traits

A young man with a graduate school education was indecisive and kept passing up job opportunities. He dreamed, "I was in an airplane that started to take off. It went down the runway but couldn't lift off." He associated the plane to himself, his indecisiveness, and his inability to start his career. He realized that he had a pattern of self-sabotage, characterized by procrastination, self-doubt, and lack of initiative. The imagery in this dream made a strong impression on him and facilitated an exploration of his self-destructive behavior.

A female teacher found herself disliked by her colleagues and students. She dreamed, "I was trying to wake up my daughter. She refused to get up and said, 'You either punish or slap everybody.' I wondered whether I was really that bad." As she reflected on the dream, she realized that she tended to be controlling and harsh. Her parents had been strict disciplinarians, and she identified strongly with them. The dream focused her on the origins of her behavior and its impact on others.

A successful businessman was constantly anxious and had no close friends. He dreamed, "I was kidnapped by some men and held captive. I was to be used as a guinea pig for some kind of experiment. I tried to figure out how to bribe the guards and to escape, but there was no one I could trust." His situation in the dream paralleled how he felt about himself: socially isolated, suspicious of others, and unable to change himself. He was particularly distrustful of other men, whom he felt might take advantage of him or hurt him in some way. His father was extremely critical and punitive while he was growing up, leading to his fear and distrust of other men. The dream enabled him to understand why he found them so threatening and frightening.

A married woman who relied excessively on the opinions of her husband and others dreamed, "I was walking in the town where I grew up. I noticed a woman about my age with a baby in her arms. It looked peaceful and secure." She associated the woman to herself and the baby to her feelings of dependency and insecurity. Her mother had been overprotective and interfered with her attempts to be more independent during her adolescence and early adulthood. She wished she could be peaceful and secure like the baby in her adult life. The dream helped her to realize that she continued to rely on her mother for a sense of security. Moreover, she endowed her husband and others with her mother's power.

Success, Recognition

A female musician felt insecure about her career and inferior to other performers. She dreamed, "I was on a TV show where I was in a piano-playing contest. The contestants were narrowed down to another woman and me. I won and asked a friend why I was chosen. He said, 'Because you're the best.'" The dream indicated not only her wish to succeed but also her inner belief in her ability to become successful. The male friend was a colleague whom she respected for his honesty and good judgment. The dream provided a boost to her self-confidence, and she became less anxious about her performances.

A female graduate student was concerned over whether or not her doctoral dissertation would be approved. She dreamed, "I was with Professor G. He told me that my dissertation was fantastic. I felt supercharged and that I could go on without him." Professor G. was her advisor, and she was apprehensive about his reaction to her dissertation. She associated him to her father, who was often critical and who told her that she would never be self-supporting. The dream encouraged her to complete her dissertation and enabled her to view her professor as a more benign, supportive authority figure.

Optimism, Confidence

A woman who was recovering from a severe depression following her divorce dreamed, "I was with my friend, Jane, on a cruise ship. We were dressed in yellow pajamas and looking for lounge chairs to sit in. I said, 'It doesn't matter where we sit, Jane, we're going to have fun.'" Jane was a good friend who had been very supportive after her divorce. She associated the color, yellow, to happiness and optimism. At the time of the dream, she was feeling much improved and looked forward to taking a vacation with her friend. The dream indicated that she was no longer clinically depressed and was capable of resuming her normal activities.

A widower who led a solitary life had the following dream: "My children and I were driving down an impossible chutelike road. They were saying to me, 'C'mon, Dad, take more chances.'" At the time of the dream, his children were encouraging him to socialize more. In fact, he had joined a church group and actually had met a woman whom he planned to ask out. But the prospect of beginning another relationship was daunting. In the dream, he was telling himself to be more courageous and to take the risk. Following the dream, he asked the woman to go out with him.

Self-Assertiveness, Self-Initiative

A man's wife frequently told him that he was too passive and submissive. He dreamed, "Sally was driving our car and a man driving another car almost hit us. I went over to his car, and he got out. I told him, 'That was really rude of you.' I felt really good about confronting him." At the time of the dream, he was thinking about confronting his doctor, who he felt had not given him enough attention on a recent visit. Moreover, he was contemplating asking his boss for a raise. His wife, Sally, was encouraging him to do so. His father had been extremely domineering and frequently intimidated him. Consequently, he became submissive and passive with other men. The dream helped him to understand the extent to which his father's domineering behavior inhibited his assertiveness with other men.

A married woman felt that her husband was emotionally withdrawn and irresponsible. She dreamed, "I was with Alan at a building project. I was the supervisor for the project, but it was a heavy responsibility. He was reluctant to participate, but I felt confident that I could accomplish it." She associated the building project to her marriage, which was in need of repair. Her husband, Alan, was a poor communicator and lacked initiative. As a result, she felt that she bore more of the responsibilities in their marriage. She had divorced her first husband, who was also unreliable, without obtaining therapy. Following this dream, she resolved to confront Alan about their marital problems and to encourage him to begin marital therapy with her.

Well-Being, Security

A woman who was mourning the death of her brother dreamed, "I was walking through a pretty town in Provence, France. The fields were green, and there were beautiful flowers. I saw my brother and felt secure and peaceful." Provence reminded her of a family vacation when she was a child and how much she enjoyed playing with her brother in the fields at a farm where they stayed. Provence was also where she had enjoyed herself while on vacation as an adult. The dream reinforced the happy memories of her relationship with her brother and helped her to work through her grief.

A woman who had a history of physical and emotional abuse by her parents dreamed, "I was in my childhood home with my husband, parents, and other family members. My parents told me that they really loved me. I felt happy and secure." At the time of the dream, her mother was dying, and she was debating whether or not to visit her. Her husband was supportive of the idea, and the dream reflected her wish for the love she never experienced with her parents, as well as hope for reconciliation with her mother. Following the dream, she did visit her mother and was able to say goodbye to her.

A young man who was socially shy and anxious in crowds dreamed, "I was snowboarding alone in the mountains. It was peaceful and I was enjoying myself." Snowboarding was his favorite sport, and he felt the most secure and happy while he was doing it. He was the youngest in his family and felt picked on by his older brother. His father had a bad temper and often yelled at him. As a result, he anticipated emotional harassment by others; he felt most secure and peaceful when he was alone. This dream occurred while he was in therapy and had developed a trusting relationship with his male therapist. Subsequently, he was able to venture out more frequently in social situations.

The previous examples illustrate various arbitrarily defined categories of dreams about the self. They collectively portray the dreamer's self-image at a particular point in life. Moreover, they emphasize how past experience and current life context are important determinants of self-identity dreams. The changing content of dreams about the self is connoted by the term *self-state dreams*; that is, the sense of self is relatively fluid, depending on the interaction of core identity with past and current experience. Clearly, self-identity cannot be separated from interpersonal relationships, feelings, and events. Since these are constantly changing, self-identity dreams may be quite variable over time. There also appears to be a self-monitoring process in dreams that may have adaptational implications. That is, dreams provide the dreamer with continuous feedback about self-experience in order to point out the necessity for change in perception or behavior. For example, the widower whose children encouraged him to take more chances was, in effect, informing himself that a change in his behavior was necessary, while the woman who saw herself as a two-headed pig realized that the greedy, vicious part of her personality required changing. On the other hand, some dreams indicate that our self-state is acceptable or even desirable. Consider, for example, the woman who was resolving her grief over her brother's death by dreaming about a happy time with him on a family vacation, or the woman who was on a cruise with her friend and looked forward to having fun; the dream informed her that she was no longer depressed. As noted earlier, the dreamer may participate undisguised in certain dreams, like the young man snowboarding alone. Sometimes, the dreamer is represented by displacements, like the woman who saw herself symbolized by the two-headed pig. In summary, dreams about the self may be honest, revealing, and informative. The dreamer may be directly portrayed in them or may be symbolized by displacements. In general, they can be used by the dreamer to initiate change in every aspect of self-functioning.

In order for therapists and clients to use dreams about the self constructively, the following steps are suggested:

1. Establish the major theme(s) of the dream. Is it a dream principally about the self?
2. Identify the individuals or characters in the dream. In particular, search for displacements of the self.
3. If one of the individuals is the client, pay particular attention to the activities, behaviors, and traits that the client displays in the dream. If they are uncharacteristic of the client, do not dismiss them out of hand.
4. Examine the other individuals or characters in the dream and the associations connected to them. If the client knows them, focus on how accurately or inaccurately they are portrayed in the dream. Try to determine if they are displacements of the client.
5. Focus on the most bizarre, inappropriate qualities or behaviors displayed by individuals in the dream, including those manifested by the client. Are they exaggerations of personality traits or physical characteristics of the client? Are they the opposite of traits or characteristics of the client?
6. Are these traits or characteristics ones that the client wishes to have or to change?
7. If the client cannot identify with any of the individuals or characteristics in the dream, continue to have the client associate to them over the next few days. The client may want to discuss it with a trusted friend or family member. That person might remind the client of someone or something that the client has not thought of or has forgotten. The therapist may also subsequently think of a relevant characteristic, trait, or behavior identified with the client.

REFERENCES

Bowlby, J. 1969. *Attachment*, Vol. 1 of *Attachment and loss*. New York: Basic Books.
——. 1973. *Separation: Anxiety and anger*, Vol. 2 of *Attachment and loss*. New York: Basic Books.
Hesse, P., and D. Cicchetti. 1982. Perspectives on an integrated theory of emotional development. In *New directions for child development: Emotional development*, ed. D. Cicchetti and P. Hesse, 3–48. San Francisco: Jossey-Bass.

Piaget, J. 1954. *The construction of reality in the child*, trans. M. Cook. New York: Basic Books.

Stern, D. N. 1985. *The interpersonal world of the infant*. New York: Basic Books.

SUGGESTED READING

Eisnitz, A. J. 1987. The perspective of the self-representation in dreams. In *The interpretations of dreams in clinical work*, ed. A. Rothstein. Monograph 3, 69–85. Madison, CT: International Universities Press.

Greenspan, S. I. 1988. The development of the ego. *J. of the American Psychoanalytic Association* 36, no. 9:3–55.

Guntrip, J. S. 1971. *Psychoanalytic theory, therapy and the self*. New York: Basic Books.

Kohut, H. 1971. *The analysis of the self*. New York: International Universities Press.

———. 1977. *The restoration of the self*. New York: International Universities Press.

Kohut, H., and E. S. Wolf. 1978. The disorders of the self and their treatment: An outline. *International J. of Psychoanalysis* 59:413–25.

Levenson, E. 1987. The purloined self. *J. of the American Academy of Psychoanalysis* 15:481–90.

Mahler, M. S., F. Pine, and A. Bergman. 1975. *The psychological birth of the human infant*. New York: Basic Books.

Stolorow, R. D., and G. E. Atwood. 1992. Dreams and the subjective world. In *Essential papers on dreams*, ed. M. R. Lansky, 272–94. New York: New York University Press.

Tolpin, P. 1983. Self-psychology and the interpretation of dreams. In *The Future of Psychoanalysis*, ed. A. Goldberg, 255–71. Madison, CT: International Universities Press.

6

Problem Solving, Decision Making

MEMORY, LEARNING, PROBLEM SOLVING, AND DECISION MAKING

An accumulating body of evidence demonstrates that dreams perform an important adaptive function in our mental life (Dallet 1973; Fosshage and Loew 1978; Palombo 1978; Cartwright 1986; Domhoff 1993; Koulack 1993; Kramer 1993; Greenberg et al. 1992; Greenberg and Pearlman 1993). That is, in addition to reflecting our feelings, interpersonal relationships, and self-identity, they are also involved in problem solving and decision making. Some of this evidence is supported by studies showing that dreaming is associated with learning (Pearlman 1979; Smith 1985, 1993). For example, rats learning to negotiate a new maze demonstrate an increase in REM sleep. By the same token, humans learning a new task or language also have an increase in REM sleep. Learning requires the use of memory in order to retain what is learned. There appear to be two types of memory involved in learning: explicit, or working, memory, and implicit, or procedural, memory (LeDoux 1994). Explicit memory occurs in the initial stages of learning a new task or body of information. It is conscious and requires our constant attention and focus. For example, learning to play tennis requires one to be very attentive to the mechanics of different strokes, such as the forehand and backhand. After constant repetition and practice, the strokes become automatic and do not require conscious attention in order to be carried out. At this point, they are part of implicit memory; that is, they are unconscious and do not require conscious attention in order to be executed. The same is true of other learned activities, such as riding a bicycle or driving a car. The acquisition and storage of information involved in explicit and implicit learning seems to be an important function of dreaming. During our waking hours, we continually receive information that we process and may or may not retain. Some investigators (Palombo 1978; Koukkou and Lehman 1993; Smith 1995; Kavanaugh 1997; Hobson 1999) believe that it is during dreaming that we transform explicit memory (waking, conscious information) into implicit memory (unconscious information). Moreover, dreaming itself uses both conscious and unconscious information to solve past or present conflicts and problems. For example, the events and experiences of the preceding day (day residue), as well as those that occurred in the distant past (and have been forgotten), are often present in the same dream. In addition to resolving past and present problems, we may also anticipate future ones and prepare for their resolution. Sometimes, present and future problem solving requires a rehearsal for future action or a decision upon which future action will be based. In a series of elegant experiments, R. Greenberg et al. (1992) demonstrated how current problems and issues are processed and resolved during dreaming. In fact, it has been demonstrated that we can actually change the course and outcome of problem solving while we dream (Cartwright 1977). Some dreams are successful in resolving problems and conflicts, while others may be unsuccessful. In either case, the dream provides us with important information about the nature of the conflict or problem and whether or not a resolution or decision can be made regarding it. In fact, the dream may be the first signal that one has resolved a problem or arrived at a decision. Sometimes, the issue is quite simple, like dreaming about an appointment one has made for the following day and does not want to forget. Or it might be much more complex, such as deciding to terminate an important relationship or to accept a new job. Regardless of the nature of the problem, we use stored information that is largely unconscious to help us resolve it or to make a decision. Of course, many problems and decisions are worked out consciously without awareness of the dream process. However, the extent to which they are worked out unconsciously in dreams indicates the adaptive function of dreaming. It appears that the problem solving and decision making accomplished in dreams allows the conscious mind more time to focus on issues that demand immediate attention. Sometimes, the issue or decision that the dream resolves is so striking and important that the dream stands out compared to other ones. These types of dreams have been termed *turning-point dreams* (Warner 1987). They may reflect a profound insight into one's personality and behavior, or they may involve a momentous decision in one's life. In fact, they can be used as reference points or bookmarkers in the chapters of one's life. An example of a decision-making and turning-point dream of historical significance was reported by President Lyndon Johnson prior to announcing that he would not run for reelection in 1968 (Goodwin 2005). In his dream, he saw himself paralyzed with a stroke, like a predecessor, Woodrow Wilson. As he was lying in his bed, he heard his cabinet secretaries outside his bedroom discussing how they would divide up his presidential duties. Upon awakening from the dream, he realized that his presidency was paralyzed because of widespread protests against the war in Viet Nam. Subsequently, he decided not to run for president again.

The following are examples of problem-solving, decision-making, and turning-point dreams:

A divorced woman was in a relationship with a man for several years. Although he loved her and demonstrated his commitment to her, she was ambivalent about marrying him. Her first husband left her for another woman, and she was deeply afraid of being rejected again. She dreamed, "I was in Chicago on a walking tour of the city. Everything seemed very real, and I was looking forward to seeing the different buildings, streets, and familiar places. I had a good feeling." She had met her first husband in Chicago, where they attended the same college. They married shortly after graduation and pursued their respective careers without ever having children. Over the ensuing years, they drifted apart emotionally and sexually. In contrast to her marriage, she felt that her current relationship was more intimate and trusting. She associated the "real" quality of her surroundings in the dream to the genuineness of the love she felt in her current relationship. Her optimism and "good feeling" as she toured the city reflected the positive attitude she experienced in this relationship as compared to her unhappiness in her marriage. Shortly after having this dream, she decided to get married. The dream demonstrated a decision-making element; it was also a turning-point dream in that it portended a major change about to take place in her life.

A divorced woman had an executive position with a corporation that was downsizing. She was also involved in an unfulfilling relationship with a married man. She dreamed, "I got on a bus in California that was heading east. I realized that I was going in the wrong direction and got off. I rented a car and headed west again. I felt relieved." She recalled that she lived in California after her divorce. During that period of her life, she had a good job and felt independent. At the time of the dream, she lived on the East Coast and felt insecure in her job, as well as unhappy in her love life. She interpreted getting off the bus and heading west as a decision to change her job and leave her boyfriend. In fact, following this dream, she broke up with her boyfriend and began dating a single man who was more appropriate for her. She also found a more secure job within her company. This dream not only involved problem solving and decision making but also represented a turning point in her life.

A single woman in her thirties remained overly dependent on her mother. The latter was extremely controlling and demanding. She dreamed, "My mother was following me from room to room, screaming. I responded to her, saying, 'Tough, but I'm getting out, anyhow.'" The image of her mother following her from room to room, screaming at her, reflected her mother's intimidating and controlling behavior. She felt that her response to her mother signified that she was no longer going to be dependent on her. It also meant that she had resolved to be more assertive with her. This was basically a problem-solving dream that reflected her decision to change her behavior with her mother.

A married businessman was insecure and frightened of his male peers. In addition, he felt that his wife was unsupportive and unsympathetic to his problems with his business competitors. He dreamed, "I was with a large man who was carrying a big box. We were trying to fit it into a particular place, and we were working together on the project. A woman was watching us, and she seemed very supportive. We succeeded in placing the box, and I felt extremely satisfied." The dreamer's father was heavy-set and often beat him. Consequently, he grew up feeling frightened of other men, especially those who were larger physically than he. Moreover, he had difficulty trusting men, in particular, his business peers and competitors. His mother did not protect him from his father, like his wife, who he felt was unsupportive. In the dream, he felt comfortable with the large man and believed that they were working together in a cooperative manner. He associated the man to his male therapist, whom he felt was helpful and encouraging. He felt that the observing woman was simultaneously his mother and his wife, who he wished had been more supportive of him. This was a problem-solving dream in which the dreamer was constructively resolving his conflict with other men. It was also a wish-fulfillment dream, insofar as he wanted the important women in his life (mother, wife) to be more supportive.

A single woman was a member of a convent for a number of years. She had taken a vow of chastity and was a virgin. However, she became depressed and entered treatment. After several years of therapy, she dreamed, "I was in an aquarium looking at some fish in a tank. Then, I noticed a necklace in the tank with a statue of a unicorn attached to it. Suddenly, I found myself swimming in the ocean and felt a sense of freedom." At the time of the dream, she was exploring her sexual identity, as well as her guilt over her sexual feelings and fantasies about men. She associated the unicorn to a mythical creature resembling a horse that symbolizes chastity and purity. However, the unicorn is also linked to sexual potency and fertility. She felt that the unicorn was symbolic of herself, conflicted over her sexual desires and self-imposed chastity. Moreover, she identified with the fish swimming freely in the tank and associated this to herself swimming freely in the ocean. Some time earlier, she had begun swimming at the YMCA and had become more comfortable wearing a bathing suit in public. She also associated swimming freely to her fantasy of leaving the convent and living independently. In fact, several months after this dream, she left the convent and subsequently began dating. A few years later, she married. In retrospect, this was a problem-solving, decision-making, and turning-point dream. At the time of the dream, it appeared to be more of a self-identity, conflict-solving one. However, it was also predictive of her later decision to leave the convent and fulfill her heterosexual desires.

A woman with several children was in an abusive marriage. She was in therapy, but her husband was opposed to it. She dreamed, "I was going on a trip with Frank [her husband], and a cab came to pick us up. I asked Frank if he had brought my luggage. He said I had to get it myself. I got angry and said I was not going on the trip with him. He left, and I put the kids in the same bed with myself." She associated the trip to their marriage and Frank's behavior in the dream to his uncooperativeness in the marriage. It is of interest that her father was abusive to her mother and that she had left home as a teenager. Her refusal to go on the trip in the dream signified her unwillingness to continue the marriage if Frank did not change his behavior. Shortly after this dream, she left her husband and took her children with her. The dream reflected her intent to resolve her conflicted marriage and was a rehearsal for her future decision to leave her husband.

A man who had a history of losing jobs and was disappointed in his career dreamed, "I had an appointment for a job interview. It was for 5 p.m., and I was in Boston. I didn't know where the street was and had to ask for directions. I was late and realized that I was sabotaging my career. I tried to hurry up." He had this dream the night before a job interview at 5:00 p.m. the following day. He had a long history of procrastination and lateness that had resulted in the loss of previous jobs. Boston was his childhood home, where he had begun a pattern of rebellious behavior toward his overly strict parents. Unfortunately, his defiant behavior included a stubbornness not to conform to the expectations of others. As a result, he often sabotaged relationships and jobs by refusing to meet his responsibilities. He realized this in the dream and tried to change his behavior by hurrying up. The dream confronted him with his self-defeating behavior and represented his attempt to begin changing it.

A young woman entered treatment because of guilt over the death of her mother. The latter was an alcoholic who died in a fire that began when she dropped a lit cigarette in her bed while drunk. The daughter felt that she ought to have been with her at the time so that she could have prevented the accident. Although she did not live with her mother, she felt responsible for her after her father had left her because of the drinking. Near the end of her therapy, she dreamed, "I was at a lake where our family vacationed when I was a child. Our family doctor was there, and I decided to swim across the lake. The doctor offered me a pair of flippers to help swim. I refused, and said I could do it on my own." The lake in the dream brought back memories of her happy childhood before her mother's alcoholism and her parents' divorce. She associated the family doctor to her therapist, who had helped her resolve her guilt over her mother's death. At the time of the dream, she felt that she had reconnected emotionally to the mother she knew and loved prior to her illness and death. This provided her with the internal strength to continue her life without a burden of guilt. Moreover, she had resolved her anger toward her father for leaving her mother. In the dream, she was telling herself that she no longer needed her therapist and had resolved her guilt and anger. The image of her decision to swim alone without help indicated her readiness to terminate treatment. When this type of dream occurs in therapy, it is referred to as a *termination dream* (Cavenar and Nash 1976; Oremland 1987; Grenell 2002) and represents a combination of problem solving, decision making, and a turning point in the dreamer's life. Therapists can use these dreams to determine whether or not a client is ready to leave treatment and function without the aid of therapy.

All of the previous examples illustrate how dreams can be useful in resolving problems or conflicts and how they can be helpful in the decision-making process. However, many dreams are neither problem-solving nor decision-making dreams; in fact, their attempts to do so are either failures or highly unrealistic and inappropriate. For example, an unhappily married man dreams that he kills his wife. Does this mean that he should kill her? Obviously, this option cannot be taken literally; however, it may mean that his anger at her has reached a murderous intensity and that a maladaptive solution has been formulated in the dream. It may also mean that he wishes to be rid of her and the problems confronting him in the marriage. Rather than carrying out the solution implied by the dream, it provides him with the opportunity to explore his options, including ways of constructively repairing the marriage. In other words, solutions and decisions presented in dreams require examination for their symbolic significance and are not necessarily to be taken literally. Therefore, it must always be kept in mind that the manifest content of a dream should be explored for its underlying meaning. In doing so, it may provide the dreamer with an opportunity to arrive at a deeper understanding of feelings, relationships, and self-perceptions evoked by the solutions and decisions appearing in the dream. Problems that end in bizarre or inappropriate solutions, that remain unresolved, or that reach an impasse in a dream offer the dreamer an avenue of exploration that may consciously lead to a constructive solution.

The following are examples of dreams concerned with problems that were not successfully resolved but provided the opportunity for constructive action.

A man who was passive and unassertive had the following dream: "I was standing with a friend in an auditorium. He tried to straighten out my stooped shoulders and told me to stand up straight. I felt humiliated and discouraged about my poor posture. However, I was unable to do as he suggested." The dreamer recalled that his parents and teachers frequently remarked on his poor posture and stooped shoulders. He associated his posture to his habit of keeping a low social profile with others. In doing so, he believed that he could avoid public notice and possible rejection. His passivity and unassertiveness also served to protect him from criticism. Although he was unable to correct his posture in the dream, it drew his attention to the reasons for his avoidant, passive behavior. The dream helped him to focus on this aspect of his personality and to begin changing it.

A female teacher felt that the teaching methods in her school were outmoded but was reluctant to discuss the issue with her principal. She dreamed, "A little boy appeared at the door of my classroom and asked to be let in. He said his name was 'Opportunity.' I told him my class was full and took him to the principal's office. As I explained the problem to the principal, I felt she wasn't listening to me, and I wouldn't be able to help him. I felt discouraged." The dreamer felt that she had a number of creative ideas to share with the principal and her fellow teachers but was afraid they would reject her. Although she had a number of opportunities to bring up her ideas at faculty meetings, she was reluctant to do so because of her fear of rejection. Her parents had repeatedly told her that she was not smart enough to go to college. Moreover, her husband often devalued her ideas and opinions. The little boy represented a part of her that wanted to take the opportunity to present her ideas. The dream pointed out her inhibition to act on her creative ideas and facilitated her exploration of the reasons she was afraid to take risks in order to express them.

A married man complained of a lack of emotional and sexual intimacy with his wife. He was afraid that if he confronted her with his feelings about their relationship, she would become angry and distance even further from him. He dreamed, "Jane and I were supposed to meet someplace. I got on a bus, but it went in the wrong direction. I was worried that I wouldn't be able to meet her at the proper place." He felt that the dream represented the different directions he and his wife were taking in their marriage. However, if he did nothing about it, there was a strong likelihood that they would never achieve the closeness he desired. He decided to discuss his feelings with his wife even though he was afraid of her negative response. To his surprise, she agreed with him, and they decided to seek marital counseling.

A woman executive worked for a company that was downsizing. Several employees in her division were laid off, and she was afraid that she would be next. She dreamed, "A forest fire was approaching my house, and I was afraid it would catch on fire. I couldn't decide what do and finally ran into the cellar to hide. I was very scared." She associated the fire to the layoffs at her company and her fear of being next. In both the dream and waking life, she felt frightened and helpless. However, the dream motivated her to talk with her supervisor about the possibility of being laid off. She was told that it was highly probable but that it would not happen for several months. This information acknowledged the reality of her situation and afforded her the opportunity to begin looking for another job.

The previous examples illustrate how dreams that do not offer solutions to problems may provide the client with information that can lead to a decision and constructive action. Frequently, the client is already consciously aware of the problem or conflict, but does not want to confront it. The dream highlights, and confronts the client with, the issue, even though there may be no resolution. Sometimes, the imagery in the dream is so dramatic (e.g., a fire) that it motivates the client to take action immediately in waking life. On the other hand, it may be more subtle and symbolic (e.g., a child named "Opportunity") but nevertheless facilitates a change in the client's attitude and behavior. In summary, dreams may present obvious decisions and solutions to problems in their manifest imagery. More often, it is the latent content that helps the client to define the problem or decision and to explore the various reasons why it remains unresolved. If this can be achieved, constructive action is possible. Whether or not a definite decision or clear resolution to a problem is accomplished, the dream can serve as a vehicle for the client to identify and explore ways of resolving the problem or arriving at a decision.

In order to help the therapist and client to understand and constructively use problem-solving and decision-making dreams, the following steps are recommended:

1. Establish whether the major theme of the dream concerns a problem or conflict that either provides or requires a resolution. Examine both the manifest and latent dream content in order to determine the nature of the problem or conflict.
2. Identify the nature of the problem or issue and determine whether it is relevant to the client's past or present life. If it is, examine the resolution or decision arrived at in the dream in order to decide if it is realistic or appropriate.
3. If the decision or solution appears realistic and appropriate, have the client discuss it further in therapy or with a trusted friend in order to re-

ceive feedback. Examine the ramifications of the decision as thoroughly as possible.

4. If the decision or solution in the dream is unrealistic, bizarre, or inappropriate, explore alternative solutions or decisions that would be more appropriate and effective. Do not interpret the manifest dream content literally.

5. If the dream offers no resolution or decision, ask why the client may be avoiding one. Explore and attempt to understand why the client is creating obstacles to resolving the problem or reaching a decision.

6. If the problem or decision seems unsolvable, it is nevertheless important for the client to continue thinking about it and to discuss it further in therapy or with a trusted friend.

7. Most significant decisions and solutions to problems are not readily apparent in dreams. However, the manifest and latent content of dreams may provide clues, ideas, memories, and feelings that might eventually help the client to arrive consciously at a resolution or decision.

REFERENCES

Cartwright, R. D. 1977. *Night life: Explorations in dreaming.* Englewood Cliffs, NJ: Prentice Hall.

———. 1986. Affect and dreamwork from an information processing point of view. *J. of Mind and Behavior* 7:411–27.

Cavenar, J. O., and J. L. Nash. 1976. The dream as a signal for termination. *J. of the American Psychoanalytic Association* 24:425–36.

Dallet, J. 1973. Theories of dream function. *Psychological Bulletin* 79:408–16.

Domhoff, W. G. 1993. The repetition of dreams and dream elements: A possible clue to a function of dreams. In *The functions of dreaming,* ed. A. Moffitt, M. Kramer, and R. Hoffmann, 293–320. Albany: State University of New York Press.

Fosshage, J., and C. Loew. 1978. *Dream interpretation: A comparative study.* New York: Spectrum Publications.

Goodwin, D. K. 2005. Personal interview on C-Span television, November 12, 2005.

Greenberg, R., H. Katz, W. Schwartz, and C. Pearlman. 1992. A research-based reconsideration of psychoanalytic dream theory. *J. of the American Psychoanalytic Association* 40:531–50.

Greenberg, R., and C. Pearlman. 1993. An integrated approach to dream theory: Contributions from sleep research and clinical practice. In *The functions of dreaming,* ed. A. Moffitt, M. Kramer, and R. Hoffmann, 363–80. Albany: State University of New York Press.

Grenell, G. 2002. The termination phase of psychoanalysis as seen through the lens of the dream. *J. of the American Psychoanalytic Association* 50:779–805.

Hobson, J. A. 1999. The new neuropsychology of sleep: Implications for psycho-analysis. *Neuro-Psychoanalysis* 1, no. 2:157–83.

Kavanaugh, J. L. 1997. Memory, sleep, and the evolution of mechanisms of synaptic efficacy maintenance. *Neuroscience* 79:7–44.

Koukkou, M., and D. Lehmann. 1993. A model of dreaming and its functional significance: The state-shift hypothesis. In *The functions of dreaming*, ed. A. Moffitt, M. Kramer, and R. Hoffmann, 51–118. Albany: State University of New York Press.

Koulack, D. 1993. Dreams and adaptation to contemporary stress. In *The functions of dreaming*, ed. A. Moffitt, M. Kramer, and R. Hoffmann, 321–40. Albany: State University of New York Press.

Kramer, M. 1993. The selective mood regulatory function of dreaming: An update and revision. In *The functions of dreaming*, ed. A. Moffitt, M. Kramer, and R. Hoffmann, 139–95. Albany: State University of New York Press.

LeDoux, J. E. 1994. Emotion, memory and the brain. *Scientific American*: 50–57.

Oremland, J. D. 1987. A specific dream in the termination phase of successful treatment. In *The interpretations of dreams in clinical work*, ed. A. Rothstein. Monograph 3, 145–54. Madison, CT: International Universities Press.

Palombo, S. R. 1978. *Dreaming and memory*. New York: Basic Books.

Pearlman, C. 1979. REM sleep and information processing: Evidence from animal studies. *Neuroscience and Biobehavioral Reviews* 3:57–68.

Smith, C. 1985. Sleep states and learning: A review of the animal literature. *Neuroscience and Biobehavioral Reviews* 9:157–68.

———. 1993. REM sleep and learning: Some recent findings. In *The functions of dreaming*, ed. A. Moffitt, M. Kramer, and R. Hoffmann, 341–62. Albany: State University of New York Press.

———. 1995. Sleep states and memory processes. *Behavior, Brain, Research* 69:137–45.

Warner, S. L. 1987. Manifest dream analysis in contemporary practice. In *Dreams in new perspective: The royal road revisited*, ed. M. L. Glucksman and S. L. Warner, 97–117. New York: Human Sciences Press.

SUGGESTED READING

DeKoninck, J., G. Proulx, W. King, and L. Poitras. 1977. Intensive language learning and REM sleep: Further results. *Sleep Research* 7:146.

Greenberg, R. 1978. If Freud only knew: A reconsideration of psychoanalytic dream theory. *International Review of Psychoanalysis* 5:71–75.

———. 1980. The private language of the dream. In *The dream in clinical practice*, ed. J. Natterson, 85–96. New York: Jason Aronson.

Smith, C., and L. Lapp. 1987. Increased number of REMs following an intensive learning experience in college students. *Sleep Research* 16:211.

Verschoor, G. J., and T. L. Holdstock. 1984. REM bursts and REM sleep following visual and auditory learning. *South African Journal of Psychology* 14:69–74.

7

Anxiety and Repetitive Dreams

DEFINITION OF ANXIETY

Anxiety is a complex emotional reaction that involves feeling, perception, physiology, and behavior. It is a ubiquitous human response to the perception of threat or danger, similar to fear. The source of the threat may be within the individual's conscious awareness, or it may be unconscious and unidentifiable. Sometimes, the distinction is made that the source of fear is conscious, while the source of anxiety is unconscious. Regardless of the source, anxiety is characterized by a subjective sense of apprehension or foreboding, along with physiological changes, including increased heart rate, elevated blood pressure, sweating, hyperventilation, and muscle tension. It is the human equivalent of the basic fight-or-flight reaction observed throughout the animal kingdom in the presence of danger. Anxiety serves as a signal that an external or internal threat exists that may cause physical or psychological harm to the person perceiving it (Freud 1900, 1926). For example, someone sailing a small craft at sea becomes aware of an approaching storm and feels anxious. In this instance, the storm is a potential physical threat to the safety of the sailor and is identifiable. By the same token, an individual beginning her first day at a job where she does not know anyone feels anxious. In this case, she may be afraid of potential rejection by her coworkers or possible embarrassment if she makes a mistake. In the foregoing examples, the individual is consciously aware of the source of the danger, and the anxiety is synonymous with fear. However, anxiety is frequently precipitated by a source that is not consciously knowable to the individual experiencing it. For example, a woman is shopping alone in a crowded store. Suddenly, she feels anxious and panicked for no apparent reason. Several more similar episodes motivate her to seek treatment. In the course of her therapy, she recalls that as a child, her mother often left her alone at home while she went to work. As she recollects her feelings during those times as a small child, she reexperiences how frightened and isolated she felt. Upon deeper exploration, she realizes that she was terrified that her mother would never return and that she would be left alone to die. The common denominator in her current and past experience is the feeling of being left alone and abandoned. Although she was subliminally aware of feeling alone in the store, she was totally unaware of the unconscious implications from her past.

Another example of an unconscious source for anxiety is the man with an executive position in a large company who begins to experience anxiety at business meetings. He becomes acutely anxious when he is presenting or explaining his reasons for a particular decision he's made. In confiding his symptoms to his brother, with whom he is quite close, he learns that his brother also has anxiety in similar situations. As they explore the problem together, they realize that their father was extremely judgmental and critical. He would often ridicule them when they gave an incorrect answer to one of his questions. As they continue their discussion, both brothers become aware of their fear of being ridiculed and humiliated if they make an incorrect decision or give a wrong answer. In this instance, the executive was not consciously aware of the source of his anxiety. Whether or not the source(s) of anxiety is consciously perceived, it is an uncomfortable feeling at the very least, and a debilitating one at the most. Sometimes, anxiety is brief and transient; at other times, it is chronic and unrelenting. A number of psychiatric disorders revolve around anxiety as the major element. These include generalized anxiety disorder, panic disorder, phobic disorder, obsessive-compulsive disorder, acute stress disorder, and posttraumatic stress disorder. In each of these disorders, anxiety or its equivalents constitute the major symptom. The source of the anxiety may or may not be conscious, but exploring and understanding its etiology are an important part of the psychotherapeutic component of treatment. Common psychogenic sources of anxiety include separation, abandonment, annihilation, physical injury, illness, death, failure, embarrassment, humiliation, criticism, and rejection.

ANXIETY AND REPETITIVE DREAMS

In view of the universality of anxiety, it is understandable that it is frequently experienced in dreams. In fact, some dreams are referred to as anxiety dreams (Freud 1900; Mack 1992). They are also commonly referred to as nightmares and are characterized by extreme fear or anxiety (Mack 1970; Hartmann 1984). Sigmund Freud believed that the biological function of dreaming is to censor or neutralize anxiety and other disturbing feelings in order that the dreamer may remain asleep. Although the available clinical and experimental evidence does not fully support Freud's theory, there are many dreams in which anxiety is not directly experienced, despite the disturbing nature of the dream content. For example, a man dreams that he is in the midst of a battlefield, yet feels detached rather than anxious. In this case, certain defense mechanisms are operating within the dream (isolation, dissociation, repression) that inhibit the anxiety. However, in numerous dreams, anxiety is either directly or indirectly felt. This occurs when the emotional regulatory function of the dream is either ineffectual or the source of the anxiety is overwhelming. The hallmark of a particular category of anxiety dreams, termed *repetitive dreams*, is the presence of anxiety (Kramer, Schoen, and Kinney 1987; Cartwright and Romanek 1978; Robbins and Houshi 1983; Domhoff 1993). These dreams are universal or common, as well as highly idiosyncratic. Examples of common repetitive dreams are those containing imagery of falling, finding oneself naked in public, feeling unprepared for an exam or speech, driving out of control without brakes, fleeing from an assailant, missing a train or plane, and engaging in an activity or performance but feeling ineffective or paralyzed. In each of these dreams, the common element is loss of control, helplessness, and anxiety. Although this type of dream seems to occur randomly, a closer examination often reveals that the dreamer is contending with a threatening situation in his or her current waking life. For example, a man has repetitive dreams of being chased at gunpoint by other men. In these dreams, he is captured and tortured or tries to escape and is caught. An examination of his waking life reveals that he is in a business partnership with several other men whom he distrusts. Moreover, he believes that they are trying to cheat him and take away his share of the business. The imagery in the dream metaphorically portrays the threatening circumstances with which he is contending. The following are further examples of repetitive anxiety dreams:

A woman has repetitive dreams in which she is driving a car down a hill and finds that her brakes are not working. The car is out of control, and she is terrified of crashing. In this instance, the dreamer is in a romantic relationship with a man who is pressuring her to marry him. She is unsure of her love for him and is afraid that if she marries him, it might lead to disaster (as her previous marriage ended in divorce).

Another woman has repetitive dreams of sitting in a classroom nude. As the other students stare at her, she feels exposed and embarrassed. In this case, the dreamer is a student teacher just beginning her classroom teaching. She is terrified of appearing incompetent and making a fool of herself.

Repetitive dreams often include physical sensations; for example, dreams of falling are very common. They may reflect neuronal activity in the cerebellum, an area of the brain that mediates balance and coordination. Other physical sensations are also frequently experienced in dreams, including erotic feelings, orgasm, the urge to urinate or defecate, suffocation, nausea, paralysis, and pain. Frequently, these sensations correlate with actual physiological processes occurring during sleep. For example, suffocation may be associated with sleep apnea. The urge to urinate in a dream usually awakens the dreamer to an actual need to urinate. Orgasms and ejaculation occur in dreams with or without imagery. Sometimes they simply express a biological urge; at other times, they are associated with imagery meaningful to the dreamer. Dreams with repetitive somatic sensations (e.g., pain) need to be evaluated in the context of the dreamer's waking life in order to determine if an actual physical cause exists. There is some evidence that physical disorders may initially manifest themselves in dream imagery (Fiss 1993). For example, a woman dreamed that she was having difficulty walking and maintaining her balance. Some time later, she became consciously aware of weakness in her legs and was diagnosed with multiple sclerosis.

POSTTRAUMATIC STRESS DISORDER AND DREAMS

Repetitive dreaming is also associated with posttraumatic stress disorder (Lansky 1990; Lansky and Bley 1995). This syndrome frequently occurs subsequent to a physical or psychological trauma. It is often found in people who have experienced a natural disaster, such as an earthquake, fire, tornado, or accident. Soldiers and civilians exposed to wartime events, including bombing, combat, prisoner of war camps, torture, and so forth, are also subject to this disorder. Individuals who have suffered a serious injury, illness, or near-death experience may also develop symptoms of posttraumatic stress disorder, which is characterized by anxiety, insomnia, preoccupation with the event (including flashbacks), and repetitive dreams that replay the experience. Psychological trauma, such as childhood sexual or emotional abuse, death of a loved one, loss of a job, academic failure, breakup of a romantic relationship, and divorce, are among the other causes of this syndrome. The frequency of the repetitive dreams is usually associated with the severity, as well as the eventual resolution, of the posttraumatic stress disorder. Sometimes, the disorder does not resolve and remains a chronic condition accompanied by repetitive dreams and flashbacks. A current theory about repetitive dreaming in posttraumatic stress disorder relates to the intensity of the anxiety associated with the traumatic experience. That is, the greater the anxiety, the less effective the dreams are in terms of regulating and diminishing it. With improvement, the anxiety is gradually diluted and the dreams become less frequent. Another possibility is that the recurrent nature of the dreams may reflect repeated attempts through dreaming to diminish the anxiety associated with the original trauma. The following are examples of repetitive dreams observed in posttraumatic stress disorder:

A woman driving her car was hit by a bus that failed to stop at a red light. She was seriously injured and spent months in the hospital, as well as in rehabilitation, recovering from her injuries. She repeatedly dreamed about the few moments prior to the accident when she saw the bus approaching her and was unable to avoid it. She felt terrified and helpless in reality, as well as in the dream. Although she became phobic of driving for months after the event, her dreams gradually diminished in frequency, and she began driving again.

A woman was treated for a malignancy with radiation and chemotherapy. She spent considerable time in the hospital and suffered from debilitating side effects. She had the following repetitive dream: "I'm lying in a hospital bed with doctors and nurses standing around me. They don't seem to know what to do, and I'm convinced I'm going to die." Indeed, she often consciously believed that her doctors could not cure her and that she would die. Over time, however, she improved, and the dreams subsided in frequency.

A man was repeatedly beaten and emotionally abused by his father during his childhood. As an adult, he suffered from chronic anxiety and insomnia. He reported the following repetitive dream: "I'm in a bedroom, and a man is standing over me with a knife in his hand. I'm afraid he's going to stab me and I try to escape. But he grabs me and starts to choke me." His symptoms persisted despite treatment, and the dream continued to recur, though with less frequency.

A woman was eating in a restaurant and swallowed some pieces of glass in her salad. She sustained lacerations inside her mouth that caused profuse bleeding. Although there was no evidence of further damage to her intestinal tract, she remained convinced that she had sustained permanent internal damage. One of her recurrent dreams was the following: "I'm on a school bus and it gets into an accident. The windshield is smashed, and all the glass goes into my mouth. I'm very upset and bleeding." She refused to eat in restaurants for a considerable period of time after the event. Following a lengthy treatment, her recurrent traumatic dreams subsided, and she was able to eat in restaurants again.

A woman who was sexually and physically abused as a child by her father and uncle had the following repetitive dream: "I'm in a dimly lit room crouching on my hands and knees. I'm held down by two men, while another one is interrogating me. My hands are tied, and I'm crying." She recalled that her father and uncle frequently held her down and tied her hands while they molested her. This dream persisted into adulthood and continued to recur despite therapy.

STRESSFUL EVENTS, ISSUES, AND DREAMS

Many anxiety dreams are not repetitive; nor are they associated with post-traumatic stress disorder. However, they are likely to occur in the context of a specific, stressful life event or circumstance. Frequently, the dreamer is consciously aware of the anxiety-producing issue, but sometimes not. Individuals often seek treatment for symptoms of anxiety or its equivalents but are totally unaware of their symptoms' source. Often, the first indication of the origin of their anxiety lies in the content of a dream. The following are examples:

An older woman entered treatment with symptoms of anxiety and insomnia. She had remarried following the death of her first husband from a chronic illness. Shortly after beginning therapy, she reported this dream: "I was in the jungle when a tiger suddenly jumped out at me. I was terrified and screamed." She associated the tiger and her terror of it to her dread of something terrible happening to her current husband, namely that he would die of an illness as her first husband had. He was the same age as her first husband when the latter was diagnosed with the illness that eventually killed him. The meaning of this dream led to her first conscious awareness of the source of her anxiety.

A newspaper reporter was unable to complete a story that he was writing. He attributed his problem to writer's block but did not experience conscious anxiety. He dreamed, "I was asked to participate in a panel discussion on a topic I knew little about. I became tongue-tied, while the other participants were extremely verbal. I felt inferior to them and worried about the audience's opinion of me." He realized that he was dissatisfied with the amount of research he had done on the topic he was writing about. In turn, he was afraid that those who read his article would be critical of it. Moreover, he worried that his fellow reporters would recognize his lack of research and lose respect for him. Of relevance was the fact that his father frequently criticized him for mistakes in his homework. In this case, writer's block was his defense against his anticipation of criticism and loss of respect. It also masked the anxiety that he would have experienced if he had been consciously aware of his concerns about the article. Being tongue-tied in the dream protected him from directly experiencing anxiety.

A middle-aged woman sought treatment for chronic anxiety, as well as feelings of inferiority and insecurity. She frequently changed jobs, claiming that she was unable to trust or get along with her female supervisors and peers. She dreamed, "I found myself in a hostile environment. Someone was trying to kill me. I was with a small child around four or five years old that I was supposed to take care of." She associated the hostile environment to her workplace, as well as to her childhood home. Her mother was extremely cruel and unaffectionate. The small child she was taking care of was herself. Her earliest memories of her mother's emotional and physical abuse extended to age four or five. She recalled feeling unprotected and vulnerable at that time. As a consequence, she grew up in a constant state of fear and distrusted other women.

Although the source of anxiety is often unknown, the dreamer is sometimes consciously aware of the event or situation promoting it. Nevertheless, a dream may serve to clarify and elaborate on the reasons for it. This information provides the dreamer with knowledge that can facilitate deeper insight and the opportunity to explore potential options in order to alleviate the anxiety. The following examples are illustrative:

An unhappily married woman dreamed, "I was on a ship, and it was fired upon. I was hit in the back with bullets and knew I was dying." Just prior to the dream, her husband had given her a birthday gift that she felt was thoughtless. It characterized his insensitivity to her needs and interests. As a result, she felt that she was dying emotionally in her marriage. The dream motivated her to confront her husband and to persuade him to enter marital counseling with her.

A male physician with an extremely busy practice dreamed, "I was immersed in a fast, rushing river. People had their arms outstretched, and I tried to grab hold of them. One man's arm broke off like papier-mâché, and I couldn't save him. I felt like I was the only person left alive in the universe and had an incredibly lonely feeling." The dreamer felt overwhelmed with his work, and several of his patients had recently died. He tended to be a loner and was unable to talk about his feelings with anyone. The dream confronted him with his social isolation and the need to share his experience with a medical colleague or friend who could be understanding and supportive.

A married woman with several children and a history of postpartum depression had recently lost her best friend to cancer. She dreamed, "I was with my husband and kids on a beach having a good time. Suddenly, a huge rattlesnake with an ugly head appeared. I was shocked and terrified." She associated the snake to her friend's death, as well as the death of her mother a few years earlier. The snake also reminded her of how terrified and despondent she felt when she was depressed. She was afraid that her friend's death might precipitate another depression and disrupt her life with her family. Following the dream, she returned to therapy in order to address her feelings about her recent losses.

An attorney who was a partner in a law firm was extremely competitive and antagonistic toward others. He dreamed, "I was a soldier in a trench on the battlefield. An officer was yelling at me to get out of the trench and kill the enemy with my bayonet. Men were being killed all around me in hand-to-hand combat." The dreamer realized that he viewed his work as military combat. He associated the officer to his father, who encouraged him to be aggressive and to win at any cost. As a consequence, he viewed professional opponents and colleagues collectively as the enemy. Because he alienated so many people with his aggressive behavior, he had no friends. The dream forced him to reassess his attitude toward others and to seek professional help.

A woman who worked long hours at her job dreamed, "I was driving over a bridge with my daughter, Kathy. The bridge began to shake, and there were potholes in the road. I was afraid we wouldn't make it over the bridge." As she thought about the dream, she realized that the many hours she devoted to her job prevented her from spending more time with Kathy. As a result, their relationship was becoming more troubled and distant. She resolved to decrease her time at work and to focus more on her relationship with her daughter.

In each of these examples, the dreamer was only vaguely aware of the problem or issue on a conscious level. Only when it was highlighted by the imagery in the dream was the dreamer able to address it with full conscious awareness. The woman with the insensitive husband knew that she was not happy in her marriage but did not become truly aware of the emotional toll it was taking on her until she was confronted by the imagery of bullets hitting her in the back and her dying. The harried physician knew he was overworked but did not realize how isolated he felt without a supportive relationship. His finding himself alone in a rushing river, unable to help anyone, was a dramatic self-confrontation in his dream. The woman who was previously depressed and grieving for her friend was unaware of how frightened she was of her depression returning. However, the image of the ugly rattlesnake focused her on her fear of both another depression and the possible death of a loved one. The aggressive attorney knew that he alienated others but was unaware of the source of his destructive competitiveness. The battlefield imagery and his commanding officer's ordering him to kill enemy soldiers confronted him with the influence of his father on his murderous competitiveness. The workaholic woman was aware of the excessive amount of time she devoted to her job but did not consciously realize how much it was eroding her relationship with her daughter. However, the imagery of a road with potholes on a shaking bridge confronted her with this deteriorating relationship.

Anxiety dreams are ubiquitous because anxiety is such a universal experience. Dreams containing other types of feelings are also quite common (e.g., sadness, guilt, anger), as was discussed in chapter 3, "Emotions or Feelings, and Mood." However, anxiety dreams often contain the most intense and dramatic imagery. The dreamer is either awakened by them (nightmares) or is more likely to recall them, in contrast to other dreams. Similar to anxiety in waking life, these dreams serve as a signal that something threatening to the dreamer demands attention. Acquiring an understanding of the meaning of the imagery in the dream enables the dreamer to address the source of the anxiety and hopefully to take the necessary steps to explore and alleviate it.

The following points are for therapists and clients to keep in mind when confronted with an anxiety dream:

1. Establish that the major feeling or emotion experienced or symbolized in the dream is anxiety or fear.
2. Explore the dream imagery and attempt to ascertain the nature of the main theme or issue. Is it connected to a past or current threat or conflict?
3. If it is a repetitive dream, examine recent or past physical and/or psychological traumas in the client's life.
4. If it is not a repetitive dream, focus on the major theme or issue and explore the current relevance it has for the client.
5. If the client believes the threat or problem is significant, explore ways to address it and, if possible, to change or correct it.
6. If the client cannot decide how to address the threat or problem, encourage him or her to explore it further in therapy and, if possible, to discuss it with a trusted friend.
7. Ascertain whether anxiety is manifested in the client's life in other ways (e.g., symptoms, mannerisms, behavior). If it is, encourage the client to explore the causes.
8. Evaluate the possible role of medication for controlling or alleviating the anxiety. In addition, rule out other disorders that may present with anxiety; for example, major depression.

REFERENCES

Cartwright, R. D., and I. Romanek. 1978. Repetitive dreams of normal subjects. *Sleep Research* 7:174.

Domhoff, G. W. 1993. The repetition of dreams and dream elements: A possible clue to a function of dreams. In *The functions of dreaming*, ed. A. Moffitt, M. Kramer, and R. Hoffmann, 293–320. Albany: State University of New York Press.

Fiss, H. 1993. The royal road to the unconscious revisited: A signal detection model of dream function. In *The functions of dreaming*, ed. A. Moffitt, M. Kramer, and R. Hoffmann, 381–418. Albany: State University of New York Press.

Freud, S. 1900. Arousal by dreams, the function of dreams, anxiety dreams. In *The standard edition of the complete psychological works of Sigmund Freud*, ed. and trans. J. Strachey, Vol. 5, 573–87. London: Hogarth Press. 1958.

———. 1926[1959]. Inhibitions, symptoms and anxiety. In *The standard edition of the complete psychological works of Sigmund Freud*, ed. and trans. J. Strachey, Vol. 20, 101–72. London: Hogarth Press.

Hartmann, E. 1984. *The nightmare: The psychology and biology of terrifying dreams*. New York: Basic Books.

Kramer, M., L. Schoen, and L. Kinney. 1987. Nightmares in Viet Nam veterans. *J. of the American Academy of Psychoanalysis* 15:67–81.

Lansky, M. R. 1990. The screening function of post-traumatic nightmares. *British J. of Psychotherapy* 6:384–400.

Lansky, M. R., with C. R. Bley. 1995. *Post-traumatic nightmares: Psychodynamic explorations*. Hillsdale, NJ: Analytic Press.

Lidz, T. 1992. Nightmares and the combat neuroses. In *Essential papers on dreams*, ed. M. R. Lansky, 323–42. New York: New York University Press.

Mack, J. 1970. *Nightmares and human conflict*. Boston: Little, Brown.

———. 1992. Toward a theory of nightmares. In *Essential papers on dreams*, ed. M. R. Lansky, 343–75. New York: New York University Press.

Robbins, P., and F. Houshi. 1983. Some observations on recurrent dreams. *Bulletin of the Menninger Clinic* 47:262–65.

SUGGESTED READING

Breger, L., I. Hunter, and R. Lane. 1971. *The effect of stress on dreams*. Psychological Issues 3, Monograph 27, 1–213. New York: International Universities Press.

DeKoninck, J. M., and D. Koulack. 1975. Dream content and adaptation to a stressful stimulus situation. *J. of Abnormal Psychology* 84:250–60.

Dowling, S. 1987. The interpretation of dreams in the reconstruction of trauma. In *The interpretations of dreams in clinical work*, ed. A. Rothstein. Monograph 3, 47–56. Madison, CT: International Universities Press.

Kellerman, H. 1987. Nightmares and the structure of personality. In *The nightmare: Psychological and biological foundations*, ed. H. Kellerman, 273–363. New York: Columbia University Press.

Stein, D. J., and E. Hollander, eds. 2002. *Textbook of anxiety disorders*. Arlington, VA: American Psychiatric Publishing.

Wright, J., and D. Koulack. 1987. Dreams and contemporary stress: A disruption-avoidance-adaptation model. *Sleep* 10:172–79.

8

Wish-Fulfillment Dreams

The element of wish fulfillment occurs with such frequency in dreams that it deserves special attention. Indeed, Sigmund Freud's (1900) central thesis was that every dream contains a wish, even though it may be camouflaged. He hypothesized that the primary function of dreams is to censor biological instincts or drives. The latter involve two basic components of human functioning: aggression and sexuality, including their derivative behaviors and mentation. By aggression, Freud meant all behavior aimed at survival, such as eating, security seeking, fighting, and exploration. Sexuality included procreation, love, affection, cooperativeness, and altruism. Generally speaking, all dreams contain elements of aggression and sexuality using this broad definition. However, not every dream is exclusively organized around a wish connected to a biological drive. Self-identity dreams, for example, often function primarily as mirrors of the self rather than as vehicles of aggressive or sexual needs. By the same token, problem-solving and decision-making dreams are not always basically connected to an instinctual need, although they do provide security or pleasure if successful. However, many dreams are primarily organized around an underlying wish and, for purposes of this discussion, are referred to as wish-fulfillment dreams.

CATEGORIES OF WISH-FULFILLMENT DREAMS

Wish-fulfillment dreams can be arbitrarily categorized according to a primary instinct (sex, aggression) or its derivatives. For example, a dream may explicitly depict a sexual need (e.g., sexual intercourse), or it may contain imagery reflecting emotional intimacy between the dreamer and someone else (a derivative behavior). In addition, the underlying wish may be either a constructive or a destructive one. For example, aggression may be expressed in the dream content by a murderous act (destructive) or by cooperating with another person on a project (constructive). Sometimes, the wish is transparent, for example, having sexual relations. At other times, it may be disguised, for example, an image from the movie *From Here to Eternity* portraying a classic love scene in the manifest content. Whether the underlying wish is obvious or disguised, constructive or destructive, the ultimate goal of the dream is to achieve a sense of security or pleasure. This is in keeping with Freud's (1917) concept of the "pleasure principal," toward which all humans aspire; that is, we constantly attempt to bring about a mental or physical state of well-being, whether awake or asleep. Wish-fulfillment dreams, in particular, reflect this process during sleep.

The following are examples of constructive wish-fulfillment dreams:

A physician in active medical practice dreamed, "I was teaching a class in medical school and interacting with the medical students. I was really enjoying it." The dreamer was a former professor in a medical school and missed his teaching activities. The dream imagery reflected his wish to return to his former professional life.

An older woman who became pregnant was concerned about her ability to have a normal baby and to care for it adequately. She dreamed, "I'm breast feeding my baby. I have plenty of milk and have a very pleasant feeling." The dream clearly portrayed her wish to be a nourishing mother with a healthy baby.

A teenage boy in high school felt awkward and insecure with his peers. He dreamed, "I was playing basketball on the school team. I was tall and scoring a lot of points. I felt pretty good." The dream is an obvious reflection of his wish to be accepted by his peers and to be seen as competent.

A man with a history of alcoholism recently joined Alcoholics Anonymous. He dreamed, "I was at a party. Someone came up to me with a tray of glasses filled with champagne and offered one to me. I refused to take it." In this instance, the dreamer is wishing to curb his impulse to drink. Whether he is able to implement this desire in waking life may be problematic.

A teacher who was up for tenure dreamed, "It was the beginning of the school year, and I was talking with my principal. He told me that I was to receive a humanitarian award and was sending me to receive it with two other teachers." The dreamer hoped to be recognized for her achievements by her boss. The humanitarian award was symbolic of tenure, as well as the qualities she wished others to recognize in her.

A man with doubts about his masculinity and effectiveness at work dreamed, "I was sitting next to an attractive woman at a party. We were having a good conversation, and I knew she liked me. At a certain point, we kissed on the lips, and I felt good about myself." At the time of the dream, he was about to have several important business meetings. The dream expresses his wish to be successful at his job and to feel sexually desired by a woman. Both sexual and aggressive needs are satisfied in this dream.

Each of the above dreams is an example of constructive wish fulfillment. The manifest content in most of them is transparent regarding the nature of the wish. However, the imagery in the dreams about wishing for tenure and to feel more effective at work is more symbolic than concrete. Some of the wishes are more realistically achievable (the teacher hoping for tenure). Others are more unrealistic (the teenager hoping to be a basketball star). The important point for the dreamer is to recognize the true nature of the wish and whether it is realistic to pursue it. Even if it is unrealistic, it may inform the dreamer of a personality characteristic or problem that deserves further examination.

The following are wish-fulfillment dreams that reflect a destructive theme:

A business executive who experienced a great deal of anxiety at work dreamed, "I was with some men who were being attacked by another group of men. One of them tried to stab me with a knife, but I grabbed it and cut his throat. I escaped but knew they would eventually find me." The wish in this dream is for self-protection in the face of mortal danger. The dreamer recalled that his father was very punitive and owned a hunting knife. As a child, he fantasized that his father might stab him as a punishment for some misdeed. This led to his constant fear of potential injury by another man, which was manifested by his anxiety in the workplace. The man whose throat he cut in the dream was a symbolic displacement of his father. Not only did this dream inform the dreamer of the source of his anxiety at work, but it also offered him the opportunity to reexamine his unrealistic perceptions of other men.

A man who felt insecure about his intellectual and athletic abilities dreamed, "John and I were riding our bikes up a steep hill. John fell off his bike, and I felt good about it. I felt superior to him and gloated over his misfortune." The dreamer's wish was to be a better cyclist than his friend. In fact, his friend John was an excellent cyclist, and the dreamer envied him. He also envied him for his professional accomplishments. Having his friend fall off his bike, then gloating over his misfortune, was a destructive wish fulfillment. It served to make the dreamer feel more competent intellectually and athletically.

A mother of several children dreamed, "Ellen wasn't listening to me. I bit her in the neck, and she screamed and cried. I felt terrible and good at the same time." The dreamer was feeling harried and frustrated taking care of her children. Ellen was her youngest daughter, who had been especially difficult on the day of the dream. The dreamer's wish was to retaliate against Ellen for the trouble she had caused. However, she also felt guilty for her aggressive behavior in the dream. She became more consciously aware of how she displayed her anger following this dream and took steps to control it.

A successful woman executive who was constantly afraid of being fired dreamed, "I was in my childhood home, and my mother was looking out the open window. She pointed out that one could fall to China. Then she fell." The dreamer recalled that her mother told her as a child that she could "fall to China." Moreover, her mother never complimented her on her successes and was basically unsupportive of her. She attributed her fear of failure and her self-doubt to her mother. In the dream, she wished her mother would fall and die for inflicting such a negative self-image on her. The "fall to China" was also symbolic of her fear of failure at work. This dream enabled her to realize the excessive influence her mother had on her self-image and her fear of failure.

A divorced woman was in conflict with her former husband over custody of their son. The divorce was precipitated by her ex-husband's addiction to drugs and his erratic behavior. Their son had serious emotional problems that were exacerbated by his father's unavailability and unpredictability. She dreamed, "I met my former husband and went to shake his hand. But it disintegrated. Other parts of his body also began to disintegrate. I felt upset and frustrated." The central wish in this dream was for her ex-husband to disappear, although there was a simultaneous wish to establish a cordial relationship (shake his hand). His physical disintegration symbolized his mental deterioration as a result of his addictive behavior, as well as the dissolution of their marriage. Moreover, it reflected her wish for him to give up the custody battle. Following this dream, the dreamer took constructive steps to work out the custody dispute with her ex-husband.

In each of the above dreams, the dreamer either directly engaged in destructive behavior or was indirectly involved when a destructive event happened to someone else. In either case, the destructive imagery reflected the dreamer's wish. The dreamer's motivations were varied and included self-protection, avoidance, envy, anger, and retaliation. Regardless of their origin, the overall purpose of the dream was to restore or maintain the dreamer's sense of security and self-esteem. Clearly, each of these wish fulfillments was inappropriate and unrealistic. However, similar to the dreams containing constructive wish fulfillments, they informed the dreamer of an underlying threat, problem, or feeling. Although they are primarily defined as wish-fulfillment dreams, they obviously contain elements of self-identity, problem solving, relationships with others, and a wide spectrum of feelings.

In summary, wish-fulfillment dreams can be constructive or destructive, realistic or unrealistic. However, they have a common purpose: that is, to provide the dreamer with a sense of security, pleasure, and well-being. More often than not, wishes cannot be detected in the manifest content. Rather, they emerge in the latent content as a result of the dreamer's free associations. Examples of wishes contained in the latent content will be provided in chapter 11, "The Interpretive Process." Whether a wish is appropriate or not, it can inform the dreamer of an issue, problem, or emotional state that may not be consciously appreciated. The dreamer can use this information to explore the meaning of the wish further in therapy, understand the motivating source, and possibly initiate corrective action.

The following steps can be helpful for the therapist and client in understanding and constructively using wish-fulfillment dreams:

1. Determine whether the manifest or latent dream imagery contains an underlying wish that is the central element of the dream.
2. If it does, identify the nature of the wish. Is it transparent? Is it symbolic?
3. Is the wish realistic or unrealistic? Is it constructive or destructive?
4. If it is realistic, constructive, and appropriate, the client can explore possible changes to initiate in his or her behavior, attitudes, relationships, and feelings that will facilitate the wish.
5. If it is unrealistic, destructive, and inappropriate, the client can explore it and decide if it is indicative of a problem, conflict, or feeling that requires further attention. In turn, this may lead to a change or modification of the client's attitudes, beliefs, feelings, or behaviors.
6. If the dream content, including the wish and its implications, is very disturbing or destructive, the therapist and client may choose to explore it further in order to assess the client's potential for acting out destructively.
7. Whether the wish is constructive or destructive, transparent or symbolic, it should always be explored for its possible latent meaning.

REFERENCES

Freud, S. 1900. The interpretation of dreams. In *The standard edition of the complete psychological works of Sigmund Freud*, ed. and trans. J. Strachey, Vols. 4 and 5. London: Hogarth Press. 1958.
———. 1917. Introductory lectures on psychoanalysis, general theory of the neuroses. In *The standard edition of the complete psychological works of Sigmund Freud*, ed. and trans. J. Strachey, Vol. 16, 356. London: Hogarth Press. 1958.

9

Life Crisis, Stress, and Dreams

DEFINITION

The term *life crisis*, or *stress*, refers to an event or problem that is threatening, catastrophic, or life changing. Examples include death of a loved one, serious illness or injury, natural disaster, divorce, job loss, bankruptcy, mental and physical abuse, or forced geographic relocation. The subjective stress experienced during any of these situations varies from individual to individual. This depends largely on the personality structure and psychological defense mechanisms employed by the person experiencing the event. Those individuals who predominantly use denial, suppression, and rationalization are more likely to experience less stress in a given situation than those who do not. The ability of individuals to cope with a life crisis depends on their character traits (e.g., stoicism, optimism, pessimism), defenses, and the severity of the crisis. Most people survive life crises and stressful events without professional help. Aside from their own emotional resources, they rely on the support of their family, friends, and community. However, if they do not possess the psychological strength to cope adequately or do not have outside support, they are vulnerable to serious consequences, including depression, acute and chronic stress disorders, psychosis, and medical illness.

Dreams that occur during life crises or significant stress fall into the same categories as previously outlined. They may be problem solving and decision making, anxiety laden, strongly emotional, repetitive, relational or self-confrontational. However, the imagery is often more dramatic and intense than usual. Although the dreamer is usually well aware of the situation, the dream may present the event or an aspect of it in a way that provides the dreamer with another perspective. This may be helpful in terms of finding more useful options to cope with the crisis. A number of investigators believe that dreams serve an adaptive function in coping with stress (Breger, Hunter, and Lane 1971; Cohen and Cox 1975; DeKoninck and Koulack 1975; Wright and Koulack 1987; Cartwright 1991; Koulack 1993). Incorporation of the stressful situation into the dream appears to be part of the process of obtaining mastery over it. Some dreams contain imagery connected to the stressful event but are devoid of the associated feelings. D. Koulack (1993) believes that dreams containing stressful material without the concomitant affect can promote mastery because the dreamer experiences the stress without being aroused by it.

Dreams may be serialized during a crisis or stressful situation, similarly to the repetitive dreams in posttraumatic stress disorder (Cartwright 1979). Over time, they may reflect improvement or working through of the event. For example, dreams following the death of a loved one may be replete with imagery connected to loss and abandonment. These themes may gradually diminish and be replaced by imagery depicting reunion with the loved one or themes of hope and renewal. In this case, the dreamer may not be consciously aware of working through a period of grieving, even though the dream imagery reflects the healing process. The difference between serial dreams in the context of a life crisis and repetitive dreams connected to a trauma (posttraumatic nightmares) is that the imagery in the latter is more representational or concrete, while that in the former is usually more symbolic and metaphorical. For example, an individual injured in an accident and suffering from posttraumatic stress disorder may have repetitive dreams of the accident itself or dreams containing imagery portraying different kinds of accidents. These will diminish in frequency as the posttraumatic stress disorder resolves. On the other hand, someone who is suddenly fired from a job may dream about the actual experience of being fired and subsequently dream of being rejected by a friend or excluded from a party. At some point, the dream imagery may change to themes of approval and acceptance if the dreamer is beginning to cope effectively with the loss of the job. Changes in dream content over time will be addressed later in chapter 10, "Changes in Dream Imagery." However, one of the most reliable methods for assessing whether someone has worked through a crisis successfully is to examine dream content during the weeks and months after the event. In summary, evidence of adaptive or maladaptive coping with a life crisis or stress is often reflected in the imagery of a single dream or a number of successive dreams.

The following are examples of dreams associated with a life crisis or stressful event:

A woman was in an emotionally abusive marriage for many years. Her husband was insensitive, cruel, and screamed at her repeatedly. He refused marital therapy, despite her repeated requests to obtain professional help. She dreamed, "I found myself swimming in a vast ocean. The waves were huge, and I was totally alone. I knew I was about to drown, and I felt helpless to save myself." She was clinically depressed and was considering suicide at the time of this dream. The dream reflected her sense of aloneness, helplessness, and fear of being overwhelmed by her feelings of despair. She also associated the waves to her husband's overpowering anger, as well to her own intense feelings of rage at him. The dream confronted her with two possibilities: either to give up and die or to take action and extricate herself from the marriage. She chose the latter course and began divorce proceedings. She was subsequently able to leave him and gain custody of her children.

A successful physician had a history of drinking heavily. At times, he was even intoxicated while seeing patients. Moreover, his marriage was in jeopardy because he spent time away from his wife drinking with others. He dreamed, "I was in my office, drunk, and sitting in my underwear. Bill came in with a group of medical students. I was embarrassed and put my pants on, but left my fly open. I tried to talk and make sense, but I couldn't because I was plastered." He was stunned by the dream imagery's portrayal of himself. For the first time in his life, he was dramatically confronted by his unprofessional and irresponsible behavior. As a consequence, he realized how vulnerable he was to professional embarrassment and humiliation. In addition, he became more consciously aware that his drinking could lead to his professional and personal demise. Shortly after this dream, he joined Alcoholics Anonymous and gave up drinking.

A professional woman became extremely depressed after her divorce and the death of her brother, both of which occurred within a short period. She became socially withdrawn, reclusive, and hopeless. She dreamed, "I was standing on a pier. There had been a nuclear holocaust, and everyone was dead. I was holding Peter in my arms, and he was dead. Jack was also dead, floating in the water, face down." The imagery of death and isolation all around her was an internal portrayal of how she felt consciously. Peter was her brother, and Jack, her husband. She felt devastated and that life was pointless after losing them. The starkness and horror of the imagery motivated her to begin treatment for her depression. After a period of taking antidepressant medication and undergoing therapy, she became more hopeful and began to socialize again.

A woman who was in treatment for feelings of depression and depersonalization, as well as for self-mutilating behavior (cutting her arms with a razor) could not remember significant periods of her childhood. After several years in therapy, she dreamed, "I was at a family party and saw a little girl crying. My parents were there, and I yelled at my father, 'Why did you hurt her so much?' I knew how I could stop the little girl from crying because I knew what was making her cry. Her father had raped her." This dream confronted the dreamer with what she had actually known consciously but had not told her therapist or fully admitted to herself—that her father had repeatedly molested her sexually from the ages of eight to fourteen. Following the dream, she was able to recall clearly instances when her father engaged in sexual intercourse with her. She never told anyone because he threatened to kill her if she did. He stopped having sex with her when she began having her periods. She kept the secret of their relationship until both parents died. Her partial amnesia about her childhood and her tendency to depersonalize were her major defenses against the painful, conscious acknowledgement of her incestuous relationship with her father. This dream was followed by other dreams and memories of her father's sexual abuse. There was sufficient consistency in her memories to validate their veracity. Over the course of treatment, she realized that her self-mutilation represented self-punishment for her incestuous behavior, as well as rage and aggression toward her father. In addition, cutting herself was a way to feel the pain of her childhood experience and to break through the absence of feeling when she was in a depersonalized state. Her self-mutilating behavior, amnesia, and depersonalization gradually diminished with treatment.

A woman who was being treated for a metastatic malignancy became depressed and suicidal. She dreamed, "I was in the hospital surrounded by my family and friends. My doctor was there, and I knew I was dying. I told my husband to take care of our children after I died." At the time of the dream, she was planning to take her own life rather than succumb to her disease. She was convinced that she was dying and wanted to avoid a painful death. However, the thought of never seeing her children again was unbearable. After this dream, she decided to fight her illness as hard as she could. She cooperated with the chemotherapy treatment and began taking yoga classes. Her malignancy went into remission, and she was able to function again as a mother.

In each of the above examples, the dreamers confronted a stressful life crisis in a dream. Although all of them were consciously aware of the crises they were facing, some element of their dream imagery helped them to gain a different perspective that enabled them to cope more effectively. In the first example, the dreamer realized it was her choice either to give up and figuratively drown or to free herself from her oppressive marriage. In the second example, the physician saw the likely possibility of embarrassment and the destruction of his career and marriage if he continued drinking. In the next example, the dreamer was dramatically confronted with her continuing isolation and despair following her divorce and the death of her brother if she did not seek treatment. In the fourth example, the dream imagery brought into sharp focus a traumatic childhood experience. This facilitated the dreamer's recall of sexual abuse and the impact it had on her adult behavior. In the final example, the dreamer's fear of never seeing her children again galvanized her to fight her illness and not give up.

In the majority of life crises, individuals neither recall their dreams nor consciously use them to address their crisis. Nevertheless, dreams connected to an individual's crisis may occur, and the dreamer works through the stress at an unconscious level. This is similar to what happens with the majority of dreams that are either forgotten or never examined. However, life-crisis dreams have the special advantage of occurring when the dreamer is particularly vulnerable, and they are often sufficiently dramatic or poignant to catch the dreamer's attention. This being the case, the dreamer can use them to gain a different perspective on the stressful situation, cope with it more effectively, or initiate action in order to change his or her circumstances. To a large extent, life-crisis dreams resemble turning-point dreams in that they offer the dreamer an opportunity to confront a stressful event and, by working through it, to obtain mastery over it.

ANNIVERSARY DREAMS

Anniversary dreams are similar to life-crisis dreams in that they mark an important event in the dreamer's life. These include death of loved ones, marriages, divorces, birthdays, graduations, holidays, and traumatic events (accidents, illnesses, disasters). The hallmark of anniversary dreams is that they occur near or on the exact date that the significant event occurred. Sometimes, they occur in the context of a life situation that reminds the dreamer of the significant event or person. They contain wish-fulfillment, problem-solving, relational, self-identity, and emotional elements. Anniversary dreams are often repetitive, similar to posttraumatic stress dreams, and they may demonstrate a change in the dreamer's perception of the event.

The following are examples of anniversary dreams:

A woman was unhappily married to her second husband. Her first marriage was to a college boyfriend who was her first love. He initiated the divorce because he felt that he had married too young and wanted to experience other relationships. On the exact date of her divorce, she dreamed, "I was with my old boyfriend [first husband] and fell in love with him again. I was college aged and very happy." This was clearly a wish-fulfillment dream in the context of an unhappy marriage and the anniversary of her divorce. It dramatically confronted her with her dissatisfaction in her current marriage and motivated her to seek marital therapy.

A woman whose parents and grandparents were no longer alive dreamed, "I was at an inn near my grandparents' home. I went inside, and my grandparents were there. I told my grandfather, 'I know you've been dead, but now you're alive again. I love you both so much and am so glad to see you again.'" The dream occurred around the anniversary of her grandfather's death. Her parents had divorced when she was nine, and for the next few years, she spent a great deal of time with her grandparents. Her mother was hospitalized several times with a serious illness, and her father was away frequently on business. Her grandparents, particularly her grandfather, provided her with a sense of security and being loved. At the time of the dream, she felt that she had been rejected by a group of her professional peers. This was a wish-fulfilling, emotionally meaningful dream that gave her a feeling of being loved and valued.

Anniversary dreams not only mark a significant event, but they also may occur in the context of a current situation or relationship that resonates with the one recalled in the dream. They exhibit the juxtaposition of present and past experience for the purpose of problem solving and conflict resolution. They may also help the dreamer to place the past event or relationship into a different or healthier perspective. In addition, they provide an emotional connection with lost loved ones, as well as with past meaningful events. In this regard, they are somewhat different from posttraumatic dreams in that they contain imagery from the past and present, while posttraumatic dreams are concerned primarily with the original trauma.

The following is an example of an anniversary dream that occurred at a significant time of the year, evoking the memory of an important relationship. The dreamer was a woman who had terminated therapy several years prior to the dream. She awoke on Thanksgiving morning from the following dream:

> I had stopped by your office with two friends of mine, a man and a woman who needed advice. Another man was seated in the waiting room, but you ushered these two friends in and began discussing their problems with them. I was on a cell phone trying to call someone when I overheard the man say something like, "That is very good advice. Thanks for helping." When I realized that the man in the waiting room could overhear everything, I got up to close the door, but it wouldn't shut. You beckoned me to come in as the couple left your office. You told me that you always had time to help people, and you had a big, happy smile. When I awoke, I had a feeling of contentment and well-being about my life in general.

The dreamer sent the following letter, including the dream, to her former therapist:

> I had this dream on Thanksgiving, and it got me to thinking about what has happened to me since I began therapy with you. I've gone back to school to become a librarian and am now working at a job I love—a lifelong dream. My husband

and I have bought a house that we share with our family and friends, and we have many happy memories here. I am enjoying music, literature, writing, and traveling. When I first met you, I was afraid to even go out of my house. I was afraid of people and thought they were out to get me or against me. I degraded myself and was afraid of being abandoned. Well, the list goes on in many other aspects of my life. In the dream, your willingness to see my friends and telling me that you always had time to help people, made me realize how you never gave up on me and always made me feel like I had potential. So, this morning, while pondering the dream, I wanted to share my thoughts with you since this is the time of year for giving thanks. When I look back on the metamorphosis in my life, I think of you as the person who taught me to cope with "the vicissitudes of life." Thanks for sharing in this remarkable transformation and have a happy Thanksgiving.

The precipitating event for this dream was Thanksgiving. The meaning of the holiday reminded the dreamer of her former therapist and her gratefulness for his help. It was also a transference dream because of the presence of her therapist in the dream imagery. Additional attention will be paid to transference dreams and their relevance to clinical change in chapter 10, "Changes in Dream Imagery."

The following steps can be taken by the therapist and client toward identifying and constructively using life crisis, stress, and anniversary dreams:

1. Determine that the client is in a life crisis or stressful situation. Examine the dream for specific feelings and imagery that highlight the crisis or event.
2. Look for elements in the imagery that are particularly meaningful and relevant (e.g., never seeing one's children again, reuniting with dead loved ones).
3. The client may take the opportunity to find another way of defining the crisis or event that offers the possibility of coping more effectively with it (e.g., acknowledging an abusive relationship or self-destructive behavior).
4. Review possible changes in perception or action that will alleviate, improve, or end the crisis (e.g., lead to changing one's attitude toward an illness or joining Alcoholics Anonymous).
5. If the dream marks the anniversary of a significant event or loss, reflect on whether there is a connection to a current situation that resonates with the original one. If there is, explore the similarities and differences in order to gain a clearer perspective on both situations.
6. An anniversary dream may provide the client with another opportunity to work through conflicted or ambivalent feelings about a past relationship

or event. It may also enable the client to view a current relationship or situation from a different perspective and to cope with it more effectively.

REFERENCES

Breger, L., I. Hunter, and R. W. Lane. 1971. *The effect of stress on dreams.* Psychological Issues No. 3, Monograph 27, 1–213. New York: International Universities Press.

Cartwright, R. D. 1979. The nature and function of repetitive dreams: A speculation. *Psychiatry* 42:131–37.

———. 1991. Dreams that work: The relation of dream incorporation to adaptation to stressful events. *Dreaming* 1:3–10.

Cohen, D. B., and C. Cox. 1975. Neuroticism in the sleep laboratory: Implications for representational and adaptive properties of dreaming. *J. of Abnormal Psychology* 84:91–108.

DeKoninck, J. M., and D. Koulack. 1975. Dream content and adaptation to a stressful stimulus situation. *J. of Abnormal Psychology* 84:250–60.

Koulack, D. 1993. Dreams and adaptation to contemporary stress. In *The functions of dreaming*, ed. A. Moffitt, M. Kramer, and R. Hoffmann, 321–40. Albany: State University of New York Press.

Wright, J., and D. Koulack. 1987. Dreams and contemporary stress: A disruption-avoidance-adaptation model. *Sleep* 10:172–79.

SUGGESTED READING

Cartwright, R. D., and L. Lamberg. 1992. *Crisis dreaming: Using your dreams to solve your problems.* New York: Harper Collins.

Dallett, J. 1973. Theories of dream function. *Psychological Bulletin* 79:408–16.

Koulack, D. 1991. *To catch a dream: Explorations of dreaming.* Albany: State University of New York Press.

10

Changes in Dream Imagery

CLINICAL AND RESEARCH FINDINGS

Dream imagery is highly variable and idiosyncratic. With the exception of repetitive dreams, the content is usually dependent on the particular day's residue, as well as the specific problems, conflicts, or emotions that concern the dreamer at the time of the dream. Nevertheless, familiar themes frequently recur with their associated conflicts and feelings. Self-identity, relationships with others, wishes, and fears that are hallmarks of the dreamer's life repeatedly appear in the dream content. However, there is an accumulating body of evidence that dream imagery connected to particular themes, self-identities, and relationships can change over time. Sigmund Freud (1905) commented on two sequential dreams of one of his patients, Dora, that revealed her changing psychodynamics. Other clinicians (Alexander 1961; Dewald 1972; Saul 1972) have noted changes in dream content over the course of treatment. S. L. Warner (1983, 1987) observed certain changes in the manifest content of successive dreams that corresponded with clinical improvement. He noted that the dream imagery became less self-punitive and more self-soothing with clinical progress. Warner (1987) also described turning-point dreams that marked a significant change in the dreamer's life and psychic functioning. W. Bonime (1962 [1982], 1986, 1991) has eloquently demonstrated how dreams reflect evolving insight and changes in the dreamer's life. M. L. Glucksman (1988) described how the manifest and latent content of successive dreams can be used to document and facilitate clinical change during treatment. More recently, Glucksman and M. Kramer (2004) reported a significant correlation between clinical change and the manifest content of selected dreams over the course of treatment. The latter research indicates that the dream may serve as a reliable instrument for the validation of clinical progress (or lack thereof) during therapy. For example, a client who suffered significant neglect and rejection by her parents in childhood had repeated themes of loss and abandonment in her dream imagery. During therapy, though, the imagery in her dreams gradually shifted to reconciliation with her parents and a greater sense of self-security. Changes in dream content over time are brought about by working through conflicts or problems in therapy, as well as maturation through life experience. On the other hand, dream content may remain static or even deteriorate if the individual does not change or becomes more mentally disturbed.

DREAMS AND PSYCHOTHERAPY

Virtually every area of functioning and self-perception can change in dream imagery over time, including feelings, relationships, self-identity, conflict resolution, and problem solving. When individuals are in treatment, dream content may also change with regard to symptoms, psychopathology, transference, defenses, relationships with others, self-image, and readiness to terminate treatment. For example, anxiety, depression, suicidal ideation, and other symptoms may appear in the dream content of clients at the beginning of treatment but subside in later dreams. Recent evidence (Kramer and Glucksman 2006) indicates that dreams in the earlier phase of treatment contain more negative or disturbed feelings than dreams that occur in the later phase of successful treatment. Conversely, there are more dreams in the later phase of successful treatment that contain positive, pleasurable feelings than in the earlier phase. Likewise, core conflicts involving abandonment, loss, rejection, rivalry, sexuality, emotional intimacy, and self-identity that are evident in the earlier phases of treatment may be resolved as treatment progresses.

Many of the functions of dreaming articulate with key components of the psychotherapeutic process. The latter includes problem solving, conflict resolution, emotional regulation, establishing meaningful connections between past and present experience, self-awareness, mastery, and adaptation. Therefore, in view of the close parallel between certain dream functions and some of the important variables of psychotherapy, it follows that dream content may reflect clinical change during treatment.

The initial dreams of therapy are particularly meaningful as they often reflect significant psychopathology, specific areas of conflict, patterns of interpersonal relationships, and self-representation (Altman 1975; Sloane 1979; Bradlow 1987). Attitudes and feelings toward the therapist in the form of positive, negative, and mixed transferences are frequently first manifested in dream imagery. Transference resolution is often similarly heralded in dream content. Therapeutic impasses and resistance to treatment are also reflected in dream imagery. Readiness to terminate therapy may be indicated by themes of autonomy, self-reliance, and less dependence on the therapist. Dreams that connote a significant change in the dreamer's psyche are synonymous with turning-point dreams. If change is solidified and permanent, subsequent dreams will confirm it. Turning-point dreams are not always positive or headed in the direction of health; they may be regressive and continue to be pathological. Whether successive dreams are in the direction of healthy or unhealthy change, they can nevertheless be used as a reliable guide to the client's progress, or lack thereof, in or out of treatment.

Manifest content itself can be a reliable guide to changes in the client's psychic functioning during the treatment process (Renik 1984; Mendelsohn 1990). For example, feelings, behaviors, relationships with others, and self-identity are often undisguised in the manifest dream imagery. Nevertheless, confirmation of clinical change, as well as the essential meaning of the dream imagery, is ultimately found in the latent content.

EARLY AND LATER DREAMS

The following are examples of a dream occurring early in treatment that reflects the client's initial symptoms, central problem, or conflict, compared to a subsequent dream of the same client later in treatment that demonstrates clinical improvement.

Early Dream: "I was in my childhood house. My mother was at the top of the stairs, and I was at the bottom. We were having an argument, and she told me she didn't love anybody except her parents. She came down after me, but I ran away. I tried to come to see you, but I couldn't find your office."

Later Dream: "You were with me at my childhood home. My husband, parents, and other family members were also there. You said that my family really loves me."

The client began treatment with feelings of anxiety and insecurity. Her central problem was that she could never be sure anyone really loved her, including her husband. Her mother, who was emotionally distant and rejecting, never told her she loved her. She had developed a positive, though somewhat ambivalent, transference toward her therapist. These elements are quite transparent in the early dream of treatment. The subsequent dream occurred after several years in therapy. It reflects an ongoing positive transference, as well as an attempt at reconciliation with her family. At this point in treatment, she was relatively symptom-free and was more trusting of her husband's love for her. She had also started visiting her parents after not seeing them for a considerable period. In addition, she was more tolerant of her mother's emotional limitations.

Early Dream: "I was escaping from some kids at school. They caught up to me and sprayed my face with paint. They told me I'd be deaf, dumb, and blind in five minutes."

Later Dream: "I was playing basketball with some guys. Everyone was very tall. I was scoring points and doing pretty well."

The client entered treatment because he was refusing to attend school. His family had made multiple moves due to his father's job, and this was a new school. He was afraid of being ridiculed and rejected by the other students. Of relevance was the fact that his older brother teased him incessantly. The early dream reflects his fear of being physically injured by the other students. The degree of injury is portrayed by his expectation of being rendered immobile and helpless. In the subsequent dream, he is participating with his peers in a competitive game and playing very well. Not only is he accepted by his teammates, but he is also performing effectively. At the time of the dream, he had returned to school and started to make friends. His self-esteem had improved, and he was beginning to stand up to his brother.

Early Dream: "I returned to teaching after a nervous breakdown. A female teacher said, 'You just made it back in time or you would have been fired.' The choir director was trying to get me to sing alone. We were in an old Victorian house. A panther was there, and I was frightened."

Later Dream: "I was at a beach resort where I won a beauty contest. I looked for my husband to tell him. I felt no urgency in finding him and savored the experience."

The client began treatment with multiple phobias and was unable to work as a teacher. She was afraid to leave her house and was concerned that she would lose her job. These issues are apparent in the early dream, including the wish to return to work. The Victorian house was her childhood home, and she associated the panther to her mother. The latter was extremely controlling and constantly warned her that the outside world was a very dangerous place. This led to a strong dependency on her mother and husband, facilitating her phobias. The choir director represented her therapist, who encouraged her to take risks and to venture out of her house. The subsequent dream occurred later in treatment, when her phobias had disappeared and she had returned to work. She was functioning more independently and thought more highly of herself. In addition, she was comfortable spending time with her friends and involved in other activities without seeking her husband's approval.

The above dreams illustrate how manifest and latent dream content can change over time in regard to symptoms, problems, conflicts, relationships, and self-identity. In each case, the client was in treatment, and successive dreams were easier to monitor by the therapist. Of course, each client's progress in treatment was also clinically evident, notwithstanding dream content. However, the earlier and later dreams of therapy served as additional confirmation of the client's progress.

Sometimes, clients do not improve or even become more disturbed while in treatment. The following are examples of this:

Early Dream: "I was going to take a civil service exam, but I wasn't allowed to do it. I started crying."

Later Dream: "I was trying to go someplace, but was blocked in every direction. I was on my lunch break from work and had lost my way. I could not get back to where I wanted to go."

The client entered treatment feeling unhappy and trapped in her job. Moreover, she was having marital problems that seemed unsolvable. The early dream reflected her emotional state, as well as her sense of being thwarted. In the subsequent dream a year later, she still felt at an impasse. Moreover, the dream imagery portrayed her feelings of futility and confusion. At the time of the subsequent dream, she had not made progress in either her job or her marriage. In addition, her unhappiness had developed into a clinical depression.

Early Dream: "I was lying in bed and felt very tired. Everything hurt, and I wondered if I would ever get up again."

Later Dream: "I was in my childhood home. My former boss was there with another man. Then, the other guy disappeared, and I asked my boss what happened to him. He replied, 'He had AIDS and died.'"

The client entered treatment for a prolonged grief reaction following the death of his companion and life partner. They had lived together for many years in a symbiotic relationship. The early dream reflected his passivity, emotional pain, and hopelessness. In the subsequent dream, there was a juxtaposition of past and present. He associated his former boss to his father, who had abandoned the family when he was a child. He was subsequently raised by his mother, who was unaffectionate and manipulative. Throughout his childhood and adult life, he felt a deep sense of emotional emptiness. His partner filled that void until he died from the complications of AIDS. Following his death, the client felt emotionally abandoned again. At the time of the later dream, he was even more depressed and hopeless.

The previous examples illustrate how dream content validated the deteriorating condition of the client. Although it was evident from the waking state of each client that there was little or no improvement during treatment, the dream content demonstrated this in a dramatic and meaningful way. Whether or not there is clinical change during treatment, dream imagery can be used as further validation of progress or lack of progress. Moreover, both therapist and client can use the dream material to explore relevant issues in order to facilitate change, especially if the therapy is at an impasse.

DREAMS AND RESISTANCE

Certain dreams occur when there are impasses or resistance to change, and these dreams provide an opportunity to explore the etiology of the opposition to change. Sometimes, such dreams occur before there is a conscious manifestation of resistance to treatment. The following example illustrates an early and later dream where resistance was a central issue in treatment:

Early Dream: "I hired someone to kill me for $7,000. I knew that I could call off my own murder at any time, but then I would lose my money. I finally called it off and lost my money."

Later Dream: "I was on a plane that was starting to take off. It gradually gathered speed as it went down the runway and finally took off."

The client was a young man who had entered treatment for procrastination and self-sabotaging behavior. Although he was extremely intelligent and held an advanced degree, his career was at a standstill because he felt paralyzed in his attempts to promote it. At the time of the early dream, therapy was at an impasse and consisted largely of rationalizations for his failures. This dream occurred just before his thirtieth birthday. Some time earlier, he had resolved to make a significant change in his life by the time he was thirty. The $7,000 was approximately the amount of money he had paid his therapist up to that point in treatment. Arranging for someone to kill him was his wish to be rid of that part of himself that was self-defeating. Murdering himself also symbolized his self-destructive behavior. The murderer represented both himself and the therapist whom he had hired to help him change. He resented paying the money and felt it was a waste because he had failed to change. Calling off his murder undermined his wish to change and represented a resistance to treatment. The imagery in the later dream symbolized a genuine motivation to change. In fact, at the time of this dream, he had started a business with a friend, which was showing signs of promise. He was also involved in a relationship with a woman whom he later married. Moreover, he was much less self-sabotaging and pessimistic about himself. The earlier dream not only validated his self-destructive behavior but also provided an opportunity for him and his therapist to explore and work through the reasons for his self-sabo-taging behavior. This led to significant changes in his career and relationships with others.

The foregoing example illustrates how resistance can be an integral part of dream content. Indeed, all dreams can be viewed as a form of resistance be-cause of the nature of the mechanisms involved in dreamwork (Gillman 1987). The metaphorical nature of symbolism, displacement, and condensa-tion disguise, to a greater or lesser extent, the true meaning of the dream. Clients often use dreams as a form of resistance during the therapy hour. For example, a client may overwhelm the therapist with a plethora of dreams dur-ing a given session, insuring that none of the dreams can be sufficiently ex-plored. On the other hand, a client may never report a dream, claiming that all dreams are either forgotten or simply do not occur. Sometimes, a client may report a dream at the very end of a session, allowing no time to examine it. At other times, a client may flood the therapist with so many associations to a dream that there is little opportunity to make sense of them. On occasion, a client will recount a dream as though it were a necessary obligation to the therapist but without genuine interest in its relevance. Frequently, a client will devalue the importance of a dream by saying, "It's just a dream" or "It's not real." Therapists need to be alert to both the appearance of resistance in dream content, as well as to the various ways that clients may use dreams as a form of resistance within the therapy hour.

TRANSFERENCE DREAMS

The relationship between client and therapist serves as a template for signif-icant relationships in the client's life. Termed the *therapeutic relationship*, it can be divided into two arbitrarily defined categories: (1) the realistic rela-tionship or working alliance, and (2) the transference (Freud 1912; Silverberg 1948; Greenson 1967; Loewald 1986; Horner 1987; Rogawski 1989). The working alliance includes perceptions, attitudes, and feelings toward the ther-apist that are realistic and appropriate on the part of the client. It also repre-sents the cooperative, reasonable aspects of the client and the helpful, ana-lyzing qualities of the therapist. The transference includes wishes, fantasies, perceptions, and feelings toward the therapist that are unrealistic or distorted on the part of the client. These elements are based on past significant rela-tionships and represent displacement and projection of aspects of those rela-tionships onto the therapist. Both parts of the therapeutic relationship can be used to facilitate change in the client's relationship with the therapist, as well as with others (Loewald 1960 [1980]; Kantrowitz, Katz, and Paolitto 1990;

Viederman 1991; Glucksman 1993). The realistic elements of the relationship foster identification by the client with the therapist's healthy, beneficial qualities. In turn, these may be internalized and integrated as part of the client's personality structure. For example, a client may identify with and internalize the therapist's empathic, nonjudgmental qualities. Likewise, transference distortions may be clarified and resolved, leading to a more realistic perception of the therapist and others. The following is an example of a transference dream:

A woman entered therapy for feelings of inadequacy and a sense of failure in her life. Early in treatment, she reported the following dream to her therapist: "You hired me to clean your house. You kept giving me books and papers to put in your office. However, your office had no door, and I could not get in. In addition, your office was filled with stacks and stacks of papers and books." The client associated to her feelings of inadequacy in therapy. She did not know what the therapist expected of her or what she should talk about. Her role as a client seemed impossible to fulfill, and she felt she could never please the therapist. Further exploration led to her relationship with her mother, who was very critical and whom she could never please. Consequently, she developed a self-image of inadequacy and an inability to satisfy others' expectations of her. In the dream, she displaced and projected her feelings about her mother onto her therapist. A major goal of therapy was to help her differentiate the therapist from her mother. Over time, clarification of her distorted perception of the therapist, as well as the realistic experience of interacting with a noncritical, nonjudgmental person, enabled her to feel less inadequate with the therapist and others.

Dream content from early and later dreams in treatment often reflects changes in the therapeutic relationship. The following examples illustrate how the content of early and later transference dreams reflects the client's working through of transference distortions, as well as his or her internalization of realistic, beneficial aspects of the therapeutic relationship:

A divorced woman entered treatment following a suicide attempt and excessive drinking. She was depressed and bitter towards her ex-husband, who left her for another woman. Her relationship with her male therapist was initially marked by distrust and anger. She was suspicious of the motives of others in general and mistrusted the intent of men and her therapist in particular. The following was an early dream in her therapy: "I was with a woman therapist, and I was furious with her. She got nasty with me and told me she was going to get me. She had short, blonde, curly hair." Her associations included two previous therapists, one of whom was a woman who resembled the therapist in the dream. She mistrusted women because she felt they were indirect and devious, like her mother. On the other hand, she believed that men could also be hurtful and untrustworthy. Her father was emotionally distant and unaffectionate. Her ex-husband betrayed her by leaving her for another woman.

She was angry with her current male psychiatrist because she felt he had misled her about the effects of the medication he had prescribed. For a significant time during treatment, she continued to be critical and distrustful of him. After several years in therapy, she related the following dream: "My father was taking me through his college campus. He was showing me the different buildings, and I felt a connection with him." At this point in her life, she was involved in a romantic relationship with a man and was feeling more secure in her relationships with other people. She was more trusting of her psychiatrist and attributed the change in her feelings for him as a result of his patience, commitment, and nonjudgmental attitude toward her. She now viewed him as a benevolent father figure who was a helpful guide in her life. A clear differentiation had developed between her psychiatrist, father, and former husband. In addition, she had internalized realistic qualities of her psychiatrist, including his support and affirmation of her. These two dreams illustrate the change from a negative to a positive transference that occurred during her therapy.

A married man was in treatment for feelings of insecurity, especially with other men. Although successful in his career, he felt anxious and vulnerable in social and business situations. He grew up with a critical, punitive father of whom he was terrified. During the initial phase of treatment, he had the following dream: "I had an appointment with you [his male therapist], but there was a snowstorm, and I arrived at your office late. You were already with another patient, but we managed to have a session. It turned out to be a lousy one. Then, you invited my wife and me to a dinner party. I felt self-conscious and awkward, although your wife was very nice to me. I was pissed off with you and didn't feel close to you." He associated to his father who was very strict and expected him to be punctual. His father always seemed to be displeased and disappointed with him. He expected the same reaction from his therapist, although he wanted to be accepted and treated as an equal. His mother was affectionate and supportive, but she was unable to protect him from his father's anger. As a result, he felt more secure with women than with men, including the therapist's wife in the dream. For a considerable time during treatment, he felt wary of, and threatened by, his therapist. Some years later, he reported the following dream: "I was in college and talking with one of my professors. He was an older man and very kind. I was flunking several classes that I had not attended. I explained to him the reasons I couldn't attend them. He listened and asked questions that made me think more about my excuses. I realized I had to go somewhere and told him I'd return. He said he would wait for me." He associated the professor to his therapist, who listened and asked questions that probed into the reasons for his behavior. The therapist's remark that he would wait reflected his patience and understanding. In contrast, his father was impatient and judgmental. At this point in treatment, he felt more secure and supported by his therapist. He had also internalized what he felt to be his therapist's realistic understanding and acceptance of him. These two dreams clearly reflect the change from a negative to a positive transference.

A divorced woman entered therapy because she felt depressed and socially isolated. Since her divorce, she had avoided relationships with men and was distrustful of others. Her mother had been physically and verbally abusive toward her, while her father was remote and indifferent. She had the following dream early in treatment: "An evil force enveloped me and followed me around. It stalked my family and looked like a person. I could not tell if it was male or female, but I knew it was evil. Then, it killed one of the children in my family." She associated the evil force to her mother who had criticized and demeaned her throughout her childhood. In addition, it reminded her of her father and ex-husband, both of whom were detached and unloving. She felt that the murdered child represented how victimized and emotionally damaged she felt. Eventually, she acknowledged that she was afraid of being psychologically controlled by her therapist, who might hurt and betray her. Several years later, she reported this dream: "I was crossing a bridge that was falling apart. A man appeared and helped me to fix it. I was able to get across it and go to a better place. The man resembled you." She associated the bridge to her life prior to therapy. Over the course of treatment, she had managed to find a better job and had begun socializing. She was also in her first relationship with a man since her divorce. Crossing the bridge symbolized the changes in her life that her male therapist had facilitated. At this point in therapy, she was much more trusting of him. She felt that he was nonjudgmental and genuinely interested in her welfare, unlike her parents and ex-husband. These two dreams from the early and later phases of treatment clearly portrayed the transition from a negative to a positive transference.

In each of these examples, the client initially had a distorted perception of the therapist based on previous relationships. However, as treatment progressed, the realistic qualities of the therapist, along with the acquisition of insight regarding the origins of distorted perceptions, enabled the client to develop a healthier, more realistic attitude toward the therapist. The resolution of transference not only led to a reality-based perception of the therapist but also to improved relationships with others. The client's early and later dreams validated this shift in transference during treatment.

INITIAL AND TERMINATION DREAMS

Evidence of significant clinical change can also be documented by comparing the first dream with the final or termination dream of treatment. It was noted in chapter 1 (see "Dreams and Psychotherapy") that the first or initial dream of treatment often contains the central conflict or problem, as well as other significant information (Altman 1975; Beratis, 1984; Bradlow 1987). The termination dream in a successful treatment provides evidence that the major problem or conflict has been resolved. It may also reflect positive changes in other aspects of the dreamer's functioning, as well as his or her capacity to separate from the therapist (Oremland 1973; Cavenar and Nash 1976; Grenell 2002).

The following are examples of initial and termination dreams in successful treatments:

Initial Dream: "I was put in a mental hospital."

Termination Dream: "I'm at an airport boarding a plane with a man. We climb up the stairs to the plane and then there are no more rungs or stairs. I'm terrified. A little girl jumps off and is killed. But I climb to safety with the man and am glad that I survived. However, I'm angst-ridden over the little girl."

The client entered treatment for volatile mood swings and a history of unstable relationships. The first dream of her treatment reflected a fear that therapy might uncover serious mental illness in her. She also associated to her sister, who had been hospitalized many times for psychotic episodes. In her final dream, she identified the little girl who was killed as a schoolmate who was actually murdered. She also identified with the little girl because of her childhood fear of being killed by her violent father. In addition, she had been suicidal prior to treatment. The man who helped her climb up the ramp to safety was her therapist, who helped her resolve the problems that stemmed from her traumatic childhood. Although remnants of her traumatic past still haunted her, she felt safer in her relationships and more self-confident.

Initial Dream: "I'm in a library or museum. A man came in and took all my jewelry. A fight ensued, and I tried to escape."

Termination Dream: "I was modeling in a fashion show with other male models. The men were from Alcoholics Anonymous. I had a good feeling."

The client entered treatment with a history of depression and alcoholism. In his initial dream of therapy, he associated the man who stole his jewelry to his male partner, who he felt was spending too much money. The museum symbolized a place where there were many historical artifacts. That reminded him of his past and his father, who was critical and demeaning. As a teenager, he had many arguments with his father and became alienated from him. He left home after high school and rarely saw his father after that. Suffering from a lack of self-esteem and self-worth, he sought love and acceptance from other men. The termination dream reflected his improved self-image. He was no longer depressed and had joined Alcoholics Anonymous. His conflicts with his male partner were largely resolved, and he had stopped drinking.

While some initial and termination dreams demonstrate clinical improvement, other dreams indicate the opposite. The following are examples:

Initial Dream: "I was on a pier holding Ben in my arms. He was dying. We were the last two people alive in the world."

Termination Dream: "I was shopping with my ex-husband. Everybody had a dog except me because mine had been run over. Its head and eyes were bloodied. I felt lonely, left out, and upset."

The client began treatment for depression after her professional partner, Ben, died. The imagery in her first dream conveyed how bereft and alone she felt. In her final dream, she continued to feel unhappy and lonely. She associated shopping with her former husband and his material acquisitiveness, which was a factor in their marital discord. The dog represented the hurt and disappointment she felt after her divorce and continued to experience. Shortly after this dream, she left treatment, depressed and unimproved.

Initial Dream: "I was trying to escape from a foreign country. It was a very repressive regime."

Termination Dream: "I was on a ship. It was fired on, and I was hit by bullets in my back. I knew I was dying."

The client began treatment because she was unhappy in her job and marriage. The foreign country represented her alienation from each, in addition to that part of herself she felt was destructive and did not understand. She also associated the repressive regime to her parents, who were distant, rigid, and unaffectionate. In the termination dream, her association to being hit in the back by bullets was to the hurt and betrayal she felt when her husband neglected to give her a card or gift for Mother's Day. She was clinically depressed at the time of the dream and believed that she was emotionally dying. Unfortunately, each of these clients failed to improve during treatment, as their initial and final dreams poignantly demonstrated.

SUCCESSIVE DREAMS

Successive dreams selected over the course of treatment may reveal emerging psychodynamic issues, as well as clinical progress. They can also facilitate collaboration between therapist and client in exploring and addressing psychodynamically meaningful material contained in the dreams. Although this information may also be obtained from conscious discourse, dreams may provide the first clues. The following example illustrates this:

A middle-aged married man entered treatment for anxiety and homosexual fantasies. He had a successful business and was well respected in his community. However, he felt his marriage lacked emotional intimacy, and he was confused about his sexual orientation. The following are five successive dreams selected at equal intervals during his treatment:

- *Dream 1*: "My store was in my father's apartment. It was Saturday night at 7 p.m. Everything was disorganized, and the merchandise was not on display. I was very anxious about how I was going to cope with this crisis."
- *Dream 2*: "You were hosting a party for me in honor of my completing an Outward Bound trip. It was at my son's fraternity house, and it was a surprise. My old friends were there, and you had photographed my life. You introduced me to your wife, and she asked me how the store was doing."
- *Dream 3*: "I was with a male robber. I tied him up and dialed 911. However, I couldn't dial it right and felt like a jerk."
- *Dream 4*: "I was in a parking lot. My wife was driving the car. A man was driving another car and almost hit us. I went over to his car and he put up his window. But he got out, and I told him, 'That was really rude of you.' I felt good about confronting him."
- *Dream 5*: "A female teacher gave me an assignment that was under water. I didn't like it and protested to her. She gave me a failing grade. I expressed my frustration to her and felt good about it."

Dream 1 was his first dream of treatment. It was very revealing about the client's personality structure and psychodynamics. His father was a major influence on him and the source of many of his conflicts. He was a successful professional who was highly critical and punitive toward the client. The latter was so frightened of his father that he often slept with a knife under his pillow because he was convinced his father might try to kill him. His mother was submissive to his father and did not protect him from his father's anger. Consequently, he grew up feeling inadequate and frightened of potential physical or psychological injury by other men. This led to a pattern of obsequious behavior toward men and a distrust of women. He was successful in his business because he made it a priority to please his customers, but he was constantly afraid of failure. The first dream introduced his conflicted relationship with his father as well as his feelings of inadequacy and fear of failure.

Dream 2 was essentially a transference dream. It reflected the client's wish to be respected and liked by the therapist. It also indicated that the client felt understood by his therapist, who had "photographed" his life. The introduction to the therapist's wife demonstrated a wish to become a member of the therapist's family. If that were the case, perhaps the therapist would be a loving father, and the therapist's wife a protective mother, in contrast to his own parents.

Dream 3 revolved around a confrontation with a male aggressor. It was precipitated by a conflict with his business partner, who he believed was cheating him. He was unsuccessful in apprehending the robber in the dream and felt similarly in his relationship with his partner. A significant number of his dreams contained themes of aggression and competition with other men. It became clear that his homosexual fantasies were attempts to seduce other men who threatened him. That is, if another man became his sexual partner, he would be less likely to hurt him. His homosexual fantasies seemed defensive in nature and connected to his terror of his father.

Dream 4 was a turning-point dream in that it was the first indication of his ability to confront a male aggressor successfully. It correlated with events in his waking life. At the time of this dream, he was able to work out a satisfactory agreement with his business partner. In addition, he was more comfortable in work-related meetings with other men. However, his relationship with his wife was still problematic. The image of her driving the car in the dream connoted her dominance in the marriage and his difficulty asserting himself with her.

Dream 5 was also a turning-point dream and reflected his ability to confront a female authority figure. Prior to this point in treatment, he shied away from arguments with his wife. Moreover, he was reluctant to confront her with his dissatisfaction regarding the lack of emotional and sexual intimacy in their marriage. However, at this time in his therapy, he was more assertive and began addressing his concerns about their marriage with her.

The above successive dreams began with a portrayal of the client's central conflict with his father, juxtaposed with his fear of men and feelings of inadequacy. Following this, he developed a positive transference, with fantasies of becoming the therapist's son. Further dreams portrayed his fear of injury by men and his inability to confront them effectively. Continued exploration and working through of this problem resulted in his becoming more assertive with men. The final dream reflected his improved assertiveness with his wife and other women.

The following is another example of successive dreams during therapy that demonstrated clinical progress:

A married woman entered treatment because of clinical depression following a number of losses in her life. Her mother was hospitalized repeatedly when she was a child for a psychiatric disorder. When she was eight, her parents divorced, and she remained with her father. However, he remarried and sent her off to boarding school as a teenager. She met and married her first husband while in college. After several years and the birth of their son, her husband became a drug addict. Their relationship was extremely chaotic until she finally divorced him. Following her graduation from college, she married her second husband. In contrast to her first husband, he was extremely stable but tended to be emotionally remote. Her son developed a psychotic illness during adolescence, requiring hospitalization and continued treatment. Despite these difficulties, she pursued her education and became a college professor. Shortly before she began treatment, her previous psychiatrist died without telling her that she was suffering from a fatal illness.

- *Dream 1*: "My husband, Ralph, was having an affair with another woman and left me."
- *Dream 2*: "I went to you for a session. I wanted to talk to you about my frustration and anxiety with work. You didn't listen, and we ended up having lunch in a restaurant. We returned to your office, and you lay down, indicating that you wanted to sleep. But I wanted to talk with you and lay down beside you. I decided to have sex with you if I couldn't talk to you. We began playing with each other, and I looked forward to having sex with you."
- *Dream 3*: "I went on a professional retreat with Alice. We shared a room together. The ground was gray with black circles. I was smoking and not sure I was allowed to, so we decided to leave. We drove away with Bob, but he was driving very fast, and I told him to slow down. I realized I'd made a mistake leaving the retreat and told Alice we had to return."
- *Dream 4*: "I was with Ralph, and he was pointing a gun at me. I told him that his passive-aggressive behavior indicated he was really hostile toward me, and he agreed. I had him arrested and put in jail. A man told me that Ralph had a great knowledge of cars. Despite that, his cars gave us a low credit rating."
- *Dream 5*: "I was in the middle of the woods with Ralph. I was supervising a building project, consisting of large brick mansions and the publication of books. One of the houses was for us. It was a heavy responsibility, but I felt confident and optimistic of the future."
- *Dream 6*: "I was with my mother in a rowboat on the water. She looked young and beautiful. I felt she was charming, mesmerizing, and witty. She was talking about her life, and I had a great feeling of love for her. My love for her was boundless, perfect, and I was extraordinarily happy."

Dream 1 introduced the client's central issue, her fear of abandonment and loss. The possibility of her husband, Ralph, leaving her for another woman was a condensation of other losses; these included her mother's disappearance when she was hospitalized, her father's remarriage, her first husband's drug problem and her subsequent divorce, her son's mental illness, her previous psychiatrist's death, and her husband's emotional remoteness.

Dream 2 centered on her transference with her therapist and her fear of being abandoned by him. In the dream imagery, he did not listen to her and wanted to sleep. Her major complaint about her husband was that he often seemed indifferent or disengaged from her. She often complained that her therapist did not understand her. In order to gain her therapist's attention in the dream, she attempted to seduce him. During her waking life, she was sexually seductive with men, beginning with her father. In her therapy sessions, she attempted to impress and figuratively seduce her therapist with her intellectual prowess. She used sexual seductiveness and intellectual proclivity in her relationships with men as defensive maneuvers in order to avoid abandonment.

Dream 3 revolved around her relationships with women and her work. Alice was a professional colleague whom she envied for her successful career. When she attended workshops and conferences, she often felt competitive and distrustful of her female peers. At the time of this dream, she had decided to leave her job because she felt constrained by the institutional rules. The image of her smoking symbolized her tendency to be outspoken and rebellious. However, she had misgivings about leaving her job and wondered whether to do so was impulsive. This was symbolized by driving too fast with her friend, Bob, who was nonconformist and a free spirit.

Dream 4 focused on her relationship with her husband, Ralph. In fact, she felt he was passive-aggressive and hostile. He was often sarcastic and made fun of her publicly. It was also difficult for him to be emotionally open and honest. She also felt that he was not a consistent financial provider. On the other hand, he was helpful in taking care of her mentally ill son and supportive in times of crisis. Over the years, she struggled with her desire to leave him and her need for his love. Although he had difficulty showing his love for her in a direct manner, there was no doubt of his commitment to her.

Dream 5 addressed her marriage and her work. At the time of this dream, she had completed a book that was about to be published. Although she was anxious about the public's response to it, she felt fairly confident and optimistic. The building project in the dream referred to her efforts to advance her career and to work on her marriage. She felt that she had matured in her field of expertise and was respected by her colleagues. She was also committed to strengthening her marriage by engaging in more joint activities with Ralph (socializing with other couples, hiking, traveling) and obtaining marital therapy.

Dream 6 was a profound turning-point dream. The imagery revolved around a reunion with her mother, who was portrayed as she remembered her in early childhood. Ever since her mother's departure, she had tried to reconnect with her by visiting her in mental hospitals and by corresponding with her. However, it was only during her mother's final illness, prior to her death, that she felt genuinely accepted and loved by her. She associated her intellectual imagination and creativity with happy childhood memories of playing with her mother. At the time of the dream, she felt more creatively spontaneous and freer than ever before. The imagery also reflected her improved self-image through her identification with her mother's charm, wittiness, and beauty.

The previous dreams chronicled the client's unfolding psychodynamics and clinical progress during treatment. The first dream introduced the central themes of loss and abandonment in her life. In the second dream, sexual seductiveness and intellectual prowess emerged as defensive maneuvers against her fear of abandonment. Her competitiveness with and distrust of women, as well as her ambivalence about leaving her job, became apparent in the third dream. Her conflicted feelings for her husband and subsequent recommitment to her marriage were prominent themes in the fourth and fifth dreams. In the final dream, she reconciled herself to her early abandonment by her mother and positively identified with her through her emerging creative spontaneity.

In the same manner that successive dreams demonstrate clinical progress during treatment, there are those that reflect a lack of progress. The following is an illustration:

An unhappily married woman entered treatment for depression and suicidal fantasies. She was married to a man with a history of job instability and sexual impotency. His frequent changes of employment necessitated multiple geographic moves that disrupted her career. This led to disappointment and anger on her part, as well as a loss of self-esteem.

- *Dream 1*: "A child was sick and throwing up. I helped it."
- *Dream 2*: "My mother was depressed, and I tried to help her."
- *Dream 3*: "I was defecating in a chair in the dining room. I looked, and it disappeared. I left."
- *Dream 4*: "I was with Jack in our first apartment. I said, 'I don't want a divorce yet. I've changed my mind.' He said, 'No, I'm leaving.' I was scared."

Dream 1 was her first dream of treatment and presented her central problem. The image of being sick and vomiting metaphorically expressed how depressed and distraught she felt. She was considering suicide as a way out of a seemingly hopeless situation. The image of a child represented dependent, immature aspects of herself. She had also considered herself ugly and a misfit as a child. However, helping the child symbolized her decision to obtain treatment in order to change her life and herself.

Dream 2 centered on her relationship with her mother, who was also depressed and had an unhappy marriage. Her mother was unaffectionate, and the dreamer was never sure of her love. Moreover, she always felt compelled to help her mother feel better. Consequently, she became the family's caregiver. She reenacted this in her marriage by catering to her husband and always placing his needs before hers. They met in college when she was an undergraduate, and he was a graduate student. Her fantasy was that he would provide a happier life for her than she had experienced with her parents.

Dream 3 was a self-state dream that symbolized her self-destructive behavior, including suicide attempts, medication abuse, and sexual affairs with inappropriate partners. This behavioral pattern resulted in feelings of disgust with herself and lack of self-worth. On the other hand, she repeatedly denied and rationalized her self-destructive acts. The image of her feces disappearing characterized her unwillingness to take responsibility for her self-destructive behavior. In therapy, she constantly challenged limits set by her therapist and developed a childlike, dependent relationship with him. This mirrored her relationship with her husband. In addition, she developed similar interactions with authority figures at work.

Dream 4 occurred when she was struggling with the decision to leave her husband, Jack. He was resistant to marital therapy and continued to be irresponsible at work, losing yet another job. In addition, he spent most of his time involved in his own activities and obsessive rituals. There continued to be a lack of sexual intimacy and affection between them. The image of their first apartment symbolized her wish that their relationship could be like it was when they were first married. She continued to be ambivalent about separating from him and was afraid that she could not survive without him. Following this dream, she finally did leave him but then became involved with several men who were psychologically abusive.

These successive dreams reflected a lack of significant progress during treatment. The initial dream introduced the client's depressed, suicidal condition, as well as her dependency and immaturity. However, she seemed motivated to change. The second dream portrayed her relationship with her mother, who was depressed and unloving. As a result, she felt like a lonely, ugly, misfit during her formative years. She idealized her future husband and hoped that he would bring her happiness. The third dream characterized her self-destructiveness, dependency, and unwillingness to acknowledge responsibility for her behavior. The final dream reflected her ambivalence over leaving her husband and her fear of not surviving without him. Although she was ultimately able to leave him, her pattern of self-destructive behavior, unsatisfactory relationships with men, and low self-esteem continued.

In summary, selected dreams during treatment can be valuable indicators of clinical progress or lack thereof. These include early and later dreams, initial and termination dreams, and successive dreams. They often provide the first reliable information about the dreamer's central conflicts, problems, feelings, relationships, and self-identity. The nature of the client's transference is often first presented in dream imagery, providing an opportunity for client and therapist to explore it. Successful resolution of the transference and significant changes in the client's other relationships are often reflected in dream content. Resistance to treatment can also be identified in dream imagery, allowing the client and therapist to explore and work through its unconscious sources. Successive dreams, especially turning-point dreams, also herald significant decisions and changes in the client's personality and behavior. These include changes in self-esteem, body image, emotional state, and relationships. Termination, or final, dreams offer evidence of the client's ability to function independently of the therapist. If significant progress has occurred, they also demonstrate successful working through of core problems and conflicts. Changes in dream content are not only limited to the successive dreams of clients in therapy. Individuals who have had the benefit of therapy, including dream analysis, can continue to monitor their dreams following termination of treatment. In turn, their dreams may reflect ongoing resolution of conflicts, changes in self-identity, vicissitudes in relationships with others, and significant life decisions. The same is true for individuals who have not had formal therapy but have learned to understand and constructively use their dreams.

The following are steps that both client and therapist can take in constructively using selected and successive dreams during treatment:

1. Examine the first, or initial, dream of treatment for information regarding central themes, problems, and conflicts. Explore the imagery for evidence of the client's self-identity, feelings, patterns of relationships, and expectations from treatment.
2. Evaluate subsequent dreams for indications of the nature of the transference. Is it positive, negative, or mixed? Is there evidence in successive dreams that the transference is becoming more positive or negative?
3. If there is an impasse or signs of resistance in therapy, examine dream material for evidence of it. Unconscious reasons for the resistance may be found in the dream content. Continue to monitor subsequent dreams for signs of resistance.

4. Take note of turning-point dreams that demonstrate successful working through of key issues or conflicts. In particular, search for evidence of change in self-image, feelings, transference, and relationships.
5. Identify decision-making dreams that portend significant changes in the client's life. Assess the realistic or unrealistic nature and appropriateness or inappropriateness of the decisions made in these dreams.
6. Evaluate termination dreams for evidence of the client's ability to function independently of the therapist. Also, determine whether there is evidence of successful working through of central problems and conflicts in termination, or final, dreams.
7. Therapists can use the content of selected and successive dreams to point out either progress or lack thereof to their clients. Certain dreams can be used as markers or reference points that highlight significant changes in the client's personality and life.
8. Clients can continue to monitor their successive dreams following treatment in order to be aware of conflict resolution, changes in self-identity, inner emotional states, interpersonal relationships, and significant decisions. The same is true for those who have not had the benefit of therapy but have learned how to understand and monitor their dreams.

REFERENCES

Alexander, F. 1961. *The scope of psychoanalysis*. New York: Basic Books.

Altman, L. L. 1975. *The dream in psychoanalysis*. New York: International Universities Press.

Beratis, S. 1984. The first analytic dream: Mirror of the patient's neurotic conflicts and subsequent analytic processes. *International J. of Psychoanalysis* 65:461–69.

Bonime, W., with F. Bonime. 1962[1982]. *The clinical use of dreams*. New York: Basic Books/DeCapo Press.

———. 1986. Collaborative dream interpretation. *J. of the American Academy of Psychoanalysis* 14, no. 1:15–26.

———. 1991. Dreams, insight and functional change. *J. of the American Academy of Psychoanalysis* 19, no. 1:124–40.

Bradlow, P. 1987. On prediction and the manifest content of the initial dream reported in psychoanalysis. In *The interpretations of dreams in clinical work*, ed. A. Rothstein. Monograph 3, 155–78. Madison, CT: International Universities Press.

Cavenar, J. O., and J. L. Nash. 1976. The dream as a signal for termination. *J. of the American Psychoanalytic Association* 24:425–36.

Dewald, P. 1972. Assessment of structural change. *J. of the American Psychoanalytic Association* 20:119–32.

Freud, S. 1905. Fragment of an analysis of a case of hysteria. In *The standard edition of the complete psychological works of Sigmund Freud*, ed. and trans. J. Strachey, Vol. 7, 7–122. London: Hogarth Press. 1958.

———. 1912. The dynamics of transference. In *The standard edition of the complete psychological works of Sigmund Freud*, ed. and trans. J. Strachey, Vol. 12, 99–108. London: Hogarth Press. 1958.

Gillman, R. D. 1987. Dreams as resistance. In *The interpretations of dreams*, ed. A. Rothstein. Monograph 3, 27–36. Madison, CT: International Universities Press.

Glucksman, M. L. 1988. The use of successive dreams to facilitate and document change during treatment. *J. of the American Academy of Psychoanalysis* 16, no. 1:47–70.

———. 1993. Insight, empathy and internalization: Elements of clinical change. *J. of the American Academy of Psychoanalysis* 21, no. 2:163–81.

Glucksman, M. L., and M. Kramer. 2004. Using dreams to assess clinical change during treatment. *J. of the American Academy of Psychoanalysis* 32, no. 2:345–58.

Greenson, R. R. 1967. *The technique and practice of psychoanalysis*. Vol. 1. New York: International Universities Press.

Grenell, G. 2002. The termination phase of psychoanalysis as seen through the lens of the dream. *J. of the American Psychoanalytic Association* 50, no. 3:779–805.

Horner, A. J. 1987. The "real" relationship and analytic neutrality. *J. of the American Academy of Psychoanalysis* 15, no. 4:491–501.

Kantrowitz, J. L., A. L. Katz, and F. Paolitto. 1990. Follow-up of psychoanalysis five to ten years after termination: II. Development of the self-analytic function. *J. of the American Psychoanalytic Association* 38, no. 3:637–54.

Kramer, M., and M. L. Glucksman. 2006. Changes in manifest dream affect during psychoanalytic treatment. *J. of the American Academy of Psychoanalysis*. 34, no. 2:249–60.

Loewald, H. W. 1960 [1980]. On the therapeutic action of psychoanalysis. In *Papers on Psychoanalysis*, 221–56. New Haven, CT: Yale University Press.

———. 1986. Transference-countertransference. *J. of the American Psychoanalytic Association* 34:275–87.

Mendelsohn, R. M. 1990. *The manifest dream and its use in therapy*. London: Jason Aronson.

Oremland, J. D. 1973. A specific dream during the termination phase of successful psychoanalysis. *J. of the American Psychoanalytic Association* 21:285–302.

Renik, O. 1984. Report on the clinical use of the manifest dream. *J. of the American Psychoanalytic Association* 32:157–63.

Rogawski, A. S. 1989. Reality in the patient-analyst relationship. *J. of the American Academy of Psychoanalysis* 17, no. 3:415–26.

Saul, L. 1972. *Psychodynamically based psychotherapy*. New York: Science House.

Silverberg, W. V. 1948. The concept of transference. *Psychoanalytic Quarterly* 17:303–21.

Sloane, P. 1979. *Psychoanalytic understanding of the dream*. New York: Jason Aronson.

Viederman, M. 1991. The real person of the analyst and his role in the process of psychoanalytic cure. *J. of the American Psychoanalytic Association* 39, no. 2:451–89.

Warner, S. L. 1983. Can psychoanalytic treatment change dreams? *J. of the American Academy of Psychoanalysis* 11, no. 2:299–316.

———. 1987. Manifest dream analysis in contemporary practice. In *Dreams in new perspective: The royal road revisited*, ed. M. L. Glucksman and S. L. Warner, 97–117. New York: Human Sciences Press.

SUGGESTED READING

Gutheil, E. A. 1951. *The handbook of dream analysis.* New York: Liveright Publishing.

Hill, C. E. 1996. *Working with dreams in psychotherapy.* New York: The Guilford Press.

Levenson, E. 1983. *The ambiguity of change.* New York: Basic Books.

Weiss, L. 1986. *Dream analysis in psychotherapy.* New York: Pergamon Press.

11

The Interpretive Process

THE COLLABORATIVE DIALOGUE AND INTERPRETATION

Dreams can be understood via either a dialogue between the dreamer and a trained listener or a self-dialogue on the part of the dreamer. The traditional process of dream interpretation during therapy takes place between the client and the therapist (Freud 1911, 1922). This is a mutually collaborative activity that requires free association and creative imagination on the part of both participants (Sloane 1979; Bonime 1986). If it is a dream group, each participant takes on the role of dreamer and therapist (Natterson 1980; Ullman 1987). However, there are certain boundaries and requirements for each role. The dreamer, of course, presents the dream and is the author of it. It is the primary responsibility of the client to free-associate to the dream imagery and to agree or disagree with the observations and interpretations of the therapist. The client is in the best position to assess whether or not a particular intervention by the therapist seems appropriate or correct. The primary responsibility of the therapist is to facilitate the client's associations. This requires empathy and intuition on the part of the therapist. The latter may carry on a parallel, internal free-associative process that leads to questions, observations, comments, or tentative interpretations. However, the client ultimately decides whether an interpretation is on the mark. Optimally, both client and therapist arrive at a mutual interpretation as a result of their collaborative effort. When the client takes the lead in arriving at an interpretation, it usually has far greater impact. In turn, this has an empowering effect, enhancing the client's ability to make decisions, change behaviors, or take actions based on the dream's meaning. An interpretation imposed on the client is usually rejected or has little impact. Interpretations offered by the therapist are likely to be most beneficial when they are tentative and left open-ended for the client to explore and elaborate on further.

Dreams may be introduced into a therapy session at any time by the client. If a dream is presented at the beginning of a session, the remainder of the hour may be taken up with associations to it. On the other hand, a dream brought up near the end of a session may have been preceded by associative material without the awareness of either the therapist or client. Often, the presentation of a dream toward the end of a session may be a form of resistance because of the lack of time left to analyze it. Dreams may also incorporate meaningful material from the preceding session or series of sessions. Entire sessions prior to and succeeding a dream may largely consist of associations to it. Sometimes, a client may overwhelm the therapist with a multitude of dreams within a session. Although these dreams may be significant, the offering of many dreams during a single session may also be, in effect, a form of resistance. Many clients never report dreams or claim not to remember their dreams. Despite continued encouragement by the therapist to write down or record their dreams or dream fragments, they remain dreamless. Most likely, such individuals utilize predominantly repressive defenses or are resistant to working with dreams. Psychotic, brain-damaged, or mentally retarded individuals may also be unable to work with dreams because of impaired cognition or diminished intellectual and abstractive capacities.

SELF-DIALOGUE AND INTERPRETATION

Self-interpretation requires that the dreamer simultaneously act as both therapist and dreamer. Free association, fantasies, memories, feelings, and interpretation constitute the self-dialogue engaged in by the dreamer. This process is usually learned either during therapy or through mentoring with someone familiar with dream analysis. Individuals who have used dream material in therapy often rely on a self-dialogue following termination to continue their self-analytic process (Kantrowitz, Katz, and Paolitto 1990; Viederman 1991). Dream diaries can also be helpful in recording and reviewing dream content over time. Self-interpretation can usually be facilitated through reference to the key elements of free association, namely themes, feelings, surroundings, activities, relationships, and self-portrayals. It may also be helpful to discuss self-interpreted dreams with a therapist or trusted friend for confirmation and additional input.

The following is an example of collaborative dream interpretation in the context of a single therapy session:

A woman schoolteacher told her therapist that she felt sleepy and depressed the day following this dream: "I was driving up a hill in the town where I grew up. There were cars parked on both sides of the road with people in them. I couldn't drive up the hill because they were parked in a manner that obstructed my path. I kept going back and forth in front of my aunt and uncle's house. I felt trapped and didn't know what to do about it. I felt tired when I woke up."

The following dialogue took place between the client and therapist after she reported the dream and her sleepy, depressed feelings subsequent to it:

Therapist: "Did the tired feeling persist all day?"

Client: "Yes. I had the day off from teaching, and no matter how hard I tried, I couldn't get what I wanted done all day."

Therapist: "What did you want to accomplish?"

Client: "I wanted to work on some school projects. I had a meeting with my principal the day before, and I didn't feel that I got my points across to her. I felt whiny and ineffective."

Therapist: "Do those feelings remind you of anything?"

Client: "Yes. They're the same feelings I had when I was a kid. I worked hard in school, but no matter how hard I tried, I couldn't improve my grades. I was fat and felt like an outsider."

Therapist: "Is that a familiar feeling for you?"

Client: "Yes. Right now, the other teachers are ahead of me in their teaching assignments, and I'm behind them. It's the same feeling I had when I was a kid in school. The other students were always ahead of me with their assignments."

Therapist: "Does that go back to the elementary school where you grew up?"

Client: "Yes. When I was in fourth or fifth grade, I felt ugly, fat, and unpopular. Sometimes, the teacher would ask me to help her with a project, and that would make me feel good. But I used to feel self-conscious when I rode my bike to play softball—fat and alone."

Therapist: "Was that the same place where you were driving the car in the dream?"

Client: "Yes, I used to ride my bike on that hill all the time. I felt awkward playing softball—too fat. My parents never came to watch me play—that made me feel bad and alone. No one ever helped me lose weight. I didn't talk to my mother about it. I couldn't talk to her about any of my feelings. I kept them to myself and pretended everything was okay, but it wasn't okay. My mother never talked to me about feelings; she just assumed I was okay. I don't feel I have the right to criticize her because she had it tough with my father, who was bedridden with arthritis."

Therapist: "It's okay to tell me about your feelings."

Client: "I remember my mom talking to another kid's mom on the telephone, saying, 'She knows more about that than I do.' I think she was talking about sex."

Therapist: "What about sex?"

Client: "I developed early. I wanted to hide my breasts. I remember when I was sick, the doctor made a house call and told me to pull down the bedcovers and take off my pajamas in order to examine me. I was embarrassed and wanted to hide. I felt there was something wrong about my lying naked in front of the doctor. I remember pretending it wasn't happening."

Therapist: "Do you remember what the doctor looked like?"

Client: "He wore glasses; his hair was thinning; maybe he was in his fifties. He was the only doctor in town and used to give us school physicals. We used to line up for him with just our underpants on. I remember him feeling my breasts. He put his whole hand on my breast and moved it around. I felt it was wrong—like a punishment. I feel squirmy now, uneasy."

Therapist: "Does the doctor remind you of anyone else?"

Client: "He was the same height as my uncle. Maybe he was a little older. I feel weird now—I have some faint sexual feelings."

Therapist: "Did they begin when you thought of your uncle?"

Client: "I always felt uncomfortable with him. He liked the ladies, and there were rumors that he played around. He wasn't nice to my aunt. He was very controlling and critical, like my ex-husband."

Therapist: "Do you recall your uncle ever looking at you in a sexual way?"

Client: "I wondered whether he ever thought about me sexually. He used to put his hand on my shoulder or pat me on my back, even when I was an adult. It made me uncomfortable."

Therapist: "Did he ever touch you in a sexual way?"

Client: "No. I can't recall any explicit sexual touching or contact. Right now, I feel trapped—I can't go any further."

Therapist: "Are you feeling trapped by me?"

Client: "No. You're trying to help me put it together, to understand what's going on."

Therapist: "What about the feeling of being trapped?"

Client: "I feel trapped a lot of times—at work—I can't transfer to another school system. I'm at a standstill in my life. I can't afford another place to live. I have the same number of friends ever since my divorce. I'm not socially outgoing. I feel trapped by my age and my physical limitations. I still feel like an outsider, like in the dream where I was separated from all the other people in their cars. I used to feel trapped with you when I couldn't get my feelings out. I feel trapped with other doctors now—that whatever is wrong with me is my fault. I felt trapped by the doctor who examined me when I was a kid. I was ashamed of my body, and I felt guilty about my sexual feelings. I felt guilty about masturbating with another girl in eighth grade. I felt guilty when I was fifteen and working as a waitress, when an older man put his arm around me and told me I was developing into a woman. I still feel guilty about my sexual feelings."

Therapist: "You feel trapped now in different parts of your life and trapped with your feelings, especially your sexual ones, just as you felt trapped as a kid."

Client: "Yes, trapped, sad, and alone."

Therapist: "Do you think when you felt sleepy and depressed the day following the dream, you were reacting to the feelings it evoked?"

Client: "Yes. I think I was trying to escape, to blot them out."

Therapist: "I think you're right."

The major theme in the manifest content of this dream was feeling trapped and ineffective. The therapist began by commenting on the tired and depressed feelings the client reported having the following day. She responded that she couldn't accomplish anything that day and had felt ineffective in a meeting with her boss the day before the dream. After the therapist asked her to elaborate on those feelings, she associated to her childhood experience of not being able to keep up with the other kids in school. She linked that with her current problem of not keeping up with the other teachers in her assignments. In addition, she commented on her self-image growing up as being fat, ugly, and unpopular. In response to the therapist's inquiry about the setting of the dream, she associated to riding her bicycle to play softball. This led to her inability to communicate her feelings to her mother, especially her embarrassment over her early sexual development.

Further associations brought up physical examinations by the doctor and her embarrassment over exposing her naked body. The therapist asked if the doctor reminded her of anybody else, perhaps to elicit transference material. She associated to her uncle, who made her feel uncomfortable because of his subliminal sexual communication with her. When the therapist pursued their relationship, she said she felt trapped and was unable to continue. Once again, the therapist brought up his own relationship with her and wondered if he made her feel trapped. She responded by talking about all the things that made her feel trapped in her life, including her work, home, social life, age, and physical limitations. She recalled her difficulty talking to the therapist about her feelings, which was similar to her inability to discuss her feelings with her mother. This appeared to be a manifestation of a maternalized transference. Following this, she returned to her sexual feelings and her guilt about them while growing up, as well as currently. The therapist made an interpretation by suggesting that she felt trapped in different parts of her life, as well as by her feelings, especially her sexual ones, in the past and present. She agreed with the interpretation and added that she felt sad and alone. The therapist wondered if her sleepiness and depression the day after the dream were connected to the feelings evoked by the dream. She replied by saying she was trying to escape from her feelings. The therapist confirmed her response by agreeing with her. This brought their collaborative dialogue full circle to the beginning of their exploration of the dream.

The foregoing example illustrates the collaborative dialogue between client and therapist. In this context, free association is an interactive process rather than a continuous monologue on the part of the client. The client brings up memories, experiences, and feelings in response to the therapist's questions. Likewise, the therapist is prompted to ask questions or make observations based on the client's responses and the therapist's associations to them. Interpretation is a mutual activity in this process: the client offers her own observations and insights as the dialogue continues, while the therapist summarizes the client's associations toward the end of the session. In this example, the collaborative effort turned out to be successful when the client confirmed the therapist's interpretive summary.

As previously noted, dreams that occur during therapy are frequently generated by material that emerges in a session or over several sessions prior to the dream. In this sense, the session or group of sessions acts as day residue for the dream. Dreams occurring between sessions may clarify and resolve the conflicts or issues being addressed at that point in treatment. They can be used by the therapist and client to facilitate insight and working through of the relevant issues.

The following example illustrates a dream that occurred between sessions and the collaborative dialogue connected to it:

A gay man sought treatment for panic attacks and a phobia of driving. He became symptomatic following a breakup with his partner, John, several years earlier. In the session prior to the dream, he explored the similarities between his partner and his father. Both gave him affection, attention, and financial support. On the other hand, both rejected him. His father left the family when the client was a teenager, and his parents subsequently divorced. Eventually, his father remarried a woman with children of her own, and he felt excluded. His partner left him for another man. In both instances, he felt abandoned, betrayed, and alone. His panic attacks began one day while he was driving in the vicinity of his childhood home. He recalled feeling alone and not in control of his life just before the attack began. As he explored the precipitants of his panic attacks, he realized that the common denominator was a feeling of aloneness and loss of control. This was usually triggered by an event or memory, frequently while driving.

The following is a portion of the dialogue between the therapist and client in the session before the dream:

Therapist: "Tell me about the similarities between your father and John."

Client: "Well, each of them left me. My father left us and got remarried. The house was sold, and we had to move. It was the one place where I felt safe."

Therapist: "Do you recall telling me how alone and abandoned you felt after your father left and you had to move?"

Client: "It's the same feeling I had when I was driving and had the panic attack."

Therapist: "Is that what you felt after your father and John left you?"

Client: "I'm feeling anxious just talking about this now."

Therapist: "What are you feeling?"

Client: "Dizzy. My voice is cracking."

Therapist: "What's going through your mind now?"

Client: "I don't want to talk about it. It's too emotional."

Therapist: "What are the feelings?"

Client: "Angry that people could do that to me."

Therapist: "Which people?"

Client: "My father and John. It's not right. They're living their lives and don't give a shit. It's not fair. I loved them."

Therapist: "Do you feel hurt?"

Client: "Big time. I feel like I felt back then, cheated and lied to."

Therapist: "Is that what you felt when you were driving and felt panicky?"

Client: "Yes. I was having memories. There's a memory connected to every place I drive. I don't know why the memories affect me that way. I'm supposed to be in control, and I'm not."

Therapist: "You've made a connection between driving through all these places and having memories that trigger different feelings."

Client: "Basically, I feel alone, nobody loves me."

Therapist: "Is that connected to feeling panicky?"

Client: "Deep down inside I knew there was a connection between my father and John. But I was afraid to admit it. I thought it meant I wanted to be sexually intimate with my father. I was confused between John and my father. Being with John was like being with my father. Sex is a way of being close to someone. John reminded me of my father—the way he held me, talked to me, did things for me."

Therapist: "In other words, John was a substitute father. Maybe even better than your father was to you."

Client: "This is like a floodgate opening up. So many things are rushing in. There are so many connections. It's weird, but good."

Therapist: "It's weird, but it's good because it helps you understand the connections."

Subsequent to this session, the client had the following dream: "I was in my childhood home in Brooklyn with my father and John. I got into an argument with my father and told him to leave. Then, I turned to John and told him I didn't want to see him again. I wanted to hug him but forced myself not to." In the next session, the following dialogue took place after the client reported this dream:

Therapist: "What do you make of telling your father and John to get out of your life in the dream?"

Client: "It wasn't working with my father. He'd tell me he was going to see me on a weekend and never show up. I don't remember my father at all. The only time I remember my father was when we worked on that car together, an old Buick. That was the best part of my life."

Therapist: "The best part of your life was working on that car with your father?"

Client: "That was just before he left. Then, he moved in with his girlfriend, and I couldn't go to visit him whenever I wanted."

Therapist: "You felt cut off from him?"

Client: "Oh, yeah. It was so brutal."

Therapist: "You wanted to do to your father what he did to you in the dream?"

Client: "Fuck yeah! But I can't hurt him. Nothing I do can hurt him. I could never hurt him the way he hurt me, never. I could never do to John what he did to me. I don't know how these two people could . . ."

Therapist: "Could what?"

Client: "How could they affect my fear of driving?"

Therapist: "Well, when you drive, you have to pass by places that remind you of them."

Client: "That's true. Every time I drive from the city to here, I pass through places that remind me of them. If my anxiety about driving is because of these two people, how do I change it?"

Therapist: "Actually, I think that's what you're doing in the dream when you try to end the relationship with each of them. By ending your relationship with them, you're trying to end the influence they have over you, the influence of those feelings of being hurt and abandoned. In a sense, it gives you more control over them. But, physically cutting off those relationships doesn't change the feelings. What you need to do is come to terms with the feelings in order to get over them."

Client: "How can feelings be so strong that they put me in this state? I know when someone dies or is raped or murdered—that can change a person's life."

Therapist: "Being abandoned or rejected, like your father did when he left the family and you couldn't see him, can have a very strong effect."

Client: "I guess he couldn't have hurt me more. He destroyed me. When he married his present wife, it happened all over again, because she came first, then her children, and my sister and I came last. But, I'm so much like him. I hate that part of me."

Therapist: "You're like him?"

Client: "I'm like him in many ways. I don't save. I buy whatever I want. He spends all his money. He made hundreds of thousands of dollars and has no money."

Therapist: "Maybe that's the way he handles his anxiety."

Client: "I do the same thing. I buy whatever makes me happy. I spend it on stupid things."

Therapist: "What do you think the reason is?"

Client: "To make me happy. But it only makes me happy for the moment."

Therapist: "What do you want to be happy about, instead of unhappy about?"

Client: "I don't know."

Therapist: "Perhaps you do it not to feel alone and abandoned."

Client: "Do you think so? I buy something not to feel alone? I don't understand the connection."

Therapist: "It helps you to feel happy for the moment. But what's your unhappiness about?"

Client: "Being alone. I'm happy playing with the thing I buy, looking at it, touching it. But that doesn't last."

Therapist: "Perhaps, the thing you buy means 'I'm not alone.'"

Client: "I never looked at it like that. I hate that part of me. I have so much shit in my house. Pile and piles, but it's mine."

Therapist: "All that shit piled in your house means 'I'm not alone.'"

Client: "It means I'm an asshole, too. Most of the things I buy I really don't like. I buy them compulsively. Some things that I buy, that I truly do like, only make me happy temporarily."

Therapist: "Perhaps, from now on when you feel the compulsion to buy something, you'll realize it's connected to this need not to be alone."

Client: "I have to work on that. I understand the connection, but I really have to think about it."

Therapist: "Things can be connected to our feelings or to people who are important in our life"

Client: "When I broke up with John, I took very few things with me. I left most of it there. I swore that I would never let that happen again. I'd never let anyone take control of my life and have my stuff. Anything I have in my life will be mine, and no one will take it away from me."

Therapist: "As I said before, you're trying to be in control in the dream by telling your father and John to leave."

Client: "I said it in my dream. I said, 'I'm taking control of this.' I said to myself, 'If I don't call him and don't hug him, I can get through this.' The dream took place in Brooklyn. Why does it take place in Brooklyn, my safe home?"

Therapist: "Perhaps because you want to get back to the safe feeling you had there before your father left the family."

Client: "I was so happy there. The one thing I remember was Sunday morning, smelling my mother's cooking. I'd go into the kitchen, and Mom was by the stove cooking. I had this wonderful, warm, safe feeling."

Therapist: "You want to have that feeling again."

Client: "If I could just find it somewhere, with someone, somehow."

Therapist: "It's warmth, safety, love, security. Those are very human needs."

Client: "I don't feel any of that now. I want to work on it."

In this example, a dream occurred between two successive sessions. The content of the session prior to the dream served as day residue. The client began the session by talking about the similarities between his father and his partner. Both rejected him, leaving him feeling abandoned and alone. He was able to connect these same feelings to his anxiety while driving. As he made this connection, he became anxious during the session. This led to his awareness of other feelings, including anger, hurt, and loss of control. At this point, the therapist observed that his anxiety while driving was connected to feeling alone and unloved. The client concluded the session by realizing that his partner was a substitute for the loving father of his childhood, who had abandoned him.

The next session began with the client recalling the dream he had between sessions. The therapist asked him to elaborate on telling his father and partner to leave in the dream. He responded by recalling the closeness he felt with his father when they worked on a car together before his father left. After both his father and partner left him, he felt cut off and betrayed. The therapist wondered if telling his father and partner to leave him in the dream was a way of ridding himself of the feelings of hurt and abandonment. He also suggested that it might be the client's way of having more control in those relationships. The client subsequently talked about his identification with his father in terms of spending money and acquiring things compulsively. The therapist suggested that acquiring things meant he was not alone. The client seemed to agree and emphatically stated that he wanted control over his life so that he would never be in the position of being left again. The therapist reiterated that he took control in the dream by telling his father and John to leave. The client wondered why the dream took place in Brooklyn and recalled the smell of his mother's cooking on Sunday mornings. He associated that experience to feelings of warmth and safety, hoping he could find them again with someone. The therapist pointed out that wanting to be safe and loved were natural human needs. The client concluded by saying he wanted to work on achieving those feelings.

This sequence of two successive sessions with an intervening dream demonstrates how a problem or conflict that emerges in one session can be incorporated into a dream that attempts to resolve the issue. In this instance, the dream was not only a problem-solving but also a relational and wish-fulfilling one. It enabled the client to work through feelings of rejection and abandonment by reversing roles and taking more control of his life. The collaborative dialogue following the dream helped him to understand the connection between his anxiety symptoms, compulsive spending, and feelings of abandonment. It concluded with his wish to establish a loving, secure relationship in the future.

SELF-INTERPRETATION

The previous illustrations are examples of a collaborative dialogue connected to a dream presented by a client during a therapy session. Since dreams occur on a nightly basis, it is both impractical and virtually impossible to have a therapist continuously available for dream interpretation. Ideally, as a result of repetitive work with dreams during therapy, the client will develop the capacity for self-interpretation.

The following are examples of dream self-interpretation by individuals who learned to free-associate and interpret their dreams in the context of therapy:

A married physician with an active medical practice was in the later stage of therapy. At this point, he was fairly adept at dream self-interpretation. His central conflict revolved around his relationship with his father, also a physician, who had died some years earlier. He felt that his father was emotionally remote and preferred his younger brother. As a consequence, he grew up questioning his self-worth and lacked self-confidence. Prior to entering private practice, he had been a professor at a medical school. He reported the following dream:

> I was a faculty member back at the medical school and was a witness to some kind of illegal activity. I was sitting in my office and heard some gunshots or witnessed some criminal act. I don't think anybody else saw it, and I felt I had to tell someone in authority. So, I went out into the hallway looking for my chairman. He was wearing a white coat, had on glasses, and seemed younger than me. I went up to him and said, "Sam, it's so good to see you." He put his arm inside mine, and we walked along arm in arm. I said, "I've got something important to share with you. Oh, you're not Sam—I thought you were my former chairman. I realize you're the present chairman. For a minute I got carried away—I thought you were somebody else."

The following are his spontaneous free associations and self-interpretation of the dream:

> After I woke up, I realized it's the first dream I had about the medical school where I taught, with Sam in it. Then it suddenly clicked—I was trying to connect with Sam. Even though it wasn't him, just saying his name was a great relief. I felt understood and validated by Sam. All the bullshit there—the pettiness, the strutting around of the academicians, their narrow-mindedness, competitiveness—all that is tolerable if you're with somebody who cares about you. If that person leaves, then the bare bones of that ugly place stand out. What I don't know is why it took me so long to have this dream. I've been gone from there for twenty-six years. Why haven't I dreamed about Sam before? I realize he's the father I never had. Why has it taken me sixty years to overcome the lack of a father? Yesterday, when I was walking my dog, I thought that when my mother and father went into a senior-care facility, we realized that my mother had been covering up his Alzheimer's disability. Not only did she cover up his Alzheimer's, but she also covered up his emotional abuse. He withheld his love from me, but he clearly loved my brother whom he validated, celebrated, and enjoyed. I, on the other hand, was a pain in the ass because I was sick all the time. I had food allergies, asthma—he even hospitalized me for treatment of

asthma one summer for a month. I have no warm memories of him, except for one time that brings tears to my eyes just thinking about it. We were at a ski lodge in Vermont, and we waxed skis together, probably for all of ten minutes one evening before we were going to ski the next day. That's the only warm moment I can remember of being with my father. The rest of it was being criticized all the time. At the end of sixth grade, I went to a bunch of parties, and he called me a "playboy." Here I was, only twelve years old, and I didn't know what that meant. I think his father called him a playboy, and he projected that onto me. He was a rebel in his own family and came to Boston to complete his medical training after he dumped a girl he was supposed to marry. About the criminal activity—maybe it was because I saw a violent movie before I had the dream. It was about a mentally ill person who had multiple personality disorder. The movie was about encounters between him as a young man and twelve adults who were all people whose personalities he had been at one time or another. They were each killed by him at different times. In the dream, I felt I had to tell somebody in authority about the crime I witnessed because I believed it was going to destroy the institution. It was some kind of rotten activity that was taking place. It reminds me of another dream I had of being back in Pittsburgh where the embers of a fire were burning underneath our house. I had another father figure in Pittsburgh, Joe, who was my chairman there. But I was kept from seeing him by his administrative assistant who jealously guarded access to him. I always had to go through her to see him. She was very smart and knew how to manipulate to get her way. I left that job because I wasn't allowed to connect with the man I thought I was going to be working for. Maybe the burning embers, the rot, the crime, represent the absence of love, the inability to connect with a father figure. When I moved here, I had another father figure at the hospital whom I respected and trusted. But he left shortly after I arrived, and I was disappointed. When I thought I saw Sam in the dream, I was happy. Just saying his name made me happy. I felt reconnected to him. Then, I realized it wasn't him; it was Don, the current chairman. I've been looking for a father. Maybe, when I went to college I was looking for a father. It was my uncle who encouraged me to go there, and he was a surrogate father. I didn't find one there—I just found drunkenness, chaos, and all my friends flunked out. It wasn't until my junior year that I moved into a single room and began enjoying some of my classes. The criminal thing at each institution I attended or worked at is that they were not nurturing, fulfilling places. They were destructive to me, ignored me, put me down. My father conveyed a sense of competitiveness to my brother and myself. I always felt I had to go to the best schools and institutions. My brother did excel at athletics and succeeded in business. As a consequence, he won my father's love and admiration. I've lived in his shadow my whole life. The son-of-a-bitch is retired now and has a home in California on the ocean. I think of him every day sitting by the ocean watching the sunset, playing golf, and buying things for his wife and his house. He always had a different personality than mine—more resilient, bouncy, funny and lighthearted. I'm like my father, I think. I have his depression. I'm sure he was depressed his whole life. It must have been great for him to relive his life through my brother's achievements and sunny personality. I always felt closer to my mother, who covered up his abuse. She tried to be a mother and a father together by giving me the love he couldn't. What does the crime mean? I guess it stands for the love I never got from my father and my disappointment with mentors and institutions. Sam was the only one I connected with, who respected and validated me. In the dream, I felt happy when I said his name and still felt okay when I realized it wasn't him. I think he's inside me now. I have to be my own father now, to do it myself.

The client began his associations by commenting on the central character in the dream, a former mentor, Sam. He felt understood and validated by Sam, who made life tolerable for him in an institution that he found unfriendly and competitive. Sam was a surrogate father, different from his own father, who was emotionally abusive, unloving, and critical. His recollection of only one warm memory of his father, when the two of them waxed skis together, was poignantly descriptive of the absence of closeness and love in their relationship. Subsequently, his associations centered on the crime that was committed in the dream. He recalled a violent movie he had seen just prior to the dream that involved multiple personalities and murder. He wondered if the crime was connected to the lack of love from his father and the inability to connect with other mentors at various jobs. At this point, he compared his brother's personality to his own. He felt that his father preferred his brother because of the latter's achievements and more buoyant personality. His own personality was similar to his father's depressive one. Feelings of envy and anger at his brother were expressed because he was the recipient of his father's love and admiration. He commented on his mother's adopting a dual personality as both mother and father in order to compensate for his father's emotional abuse. Finally, he associated again to Sam and the crime in the dream. Sam was the surrogate father who respected and supported him. The crime was symbolic of the lack of love from his father, as well as his inability to connect with other mentors and his disappointment with institutions. In conclusion, he believed that Sam was inside himself and that he could continue to provide himself with validation and self-respect.

This could be categorized as a turning-point dream because the client realized he had internalized qualities of his surrogate father, Sam. His understanding and validation enabled the client to continue providing his own self-nurturing and self-respect. The dream could also be categorized as relational and self-representational. It is entirely possible that Sam was a displacement of his therapist (transference dream), although he never associated to that relationship. A variety of feelings were experienced in the context of relationships in the dream and his associations to them. He felt a sense of well-being and relief when he saw Sam and associated loss of love, lack of respect, and disappointment to his father. Envy and anger were connected with his brother. However, he did not pursue the violence and murder that occurred in the movie he saw prior to the dream. It is possible that the crime referred to in the dream symbolized not only his father's emotional abuse but also his own murderous rage toward his father and brother. However, this is speculative and could only have been confirmed by the client through his associations. Nevertheless, the client was able to interpret the essential meaning of the dream; that is, his feelings of grief and resentment over the lack of love and connection with his father were replaced by a developing capacity within himself for self-love and self-validation. If the client had confirmed the possible transference elements of this dream, his developing capacity for self-love and self-validation would most likely have reflected an internalization of his therapist's beneficial qualities, as well as his positive feelings for the therapist.

The following is another illustration of dream self-interpretation by a woman who was in therapy and at a transition point in her life. She was a professional writer struggling with the completion of a novel. Moreover, she was ambivalent about her current marriage. A previous marriage had ended in divorce, and her early childhood was marked by her mother's mental illness. She reported the following dream:

> I was in a room with Frank Sinatra. He was alive and electric. I was aware that he had several marriages and wives. He was very focused on each wife when he was married to her, but then he would abruptly break off the marriage. I was a combination of roles in his life. I started out being his valet and son in the dream. At a certain point, he wanted me to help him stabilize a new marriage. Although I felt an obligation to him, I told him I couldn't be responsible for his situation. I said, "You live a very distracted life, and you're not able to focus. You move from one person to another, and I can't solve all this." I seemed to be playing these roles of being his child, son, valet, caretaker, and psychiatrist. Yet, at the same time, I was trying to give him the message that he had to get his own life in order. Toward the end of the dream, there was some complex stuff about going out and getting all kinds of unusual fabrics of high quality in order to make a wardrobe for him. I was caught up in the materials or fabrics and how to make the wardrobe. At the same time, I made a caveat or declaration to him that he had to live his own life and that I had to have a life of my own.

The following are her spontaneous free associations and self-interpretation of the dream:

> A former boyfriend of mine, Bob, always liked Frank Sinatra. Whenever I was with him, he would have a Sinatra recording on in the background. I never paid that much attention to Frank Sinatra before, but I especially remember a song called "Yellow Days." I just felt a stab in my heart remembering how Bob was

so focused on me when I was with him. I realize that in the book I'm writing, I'm trying to create for the reader what it's like to be the subject of that depth and focus by another person. My book is about reaching that state and what that state is like. That song was melancholy and nostalgic, with a sense of loss. I just celebrated my birthday, and one way or another, I heard from every man who had ever been important to me, including Bob. I realize that what's been driving me nuts, making me feel angry and unfulfilled—no matter how hard I work and how many people I pile into my life to try and satisfy myself, it's my husband's distractibility. We were in a shop the other day, and some beautiful music was playing. I just wanted to listen to it and be in that moment. My husband said, "Come on. Let's get going. Let's get out of here." I realize that's at the core of the problem with him and why I had a dream about Frank Sinatra. He loves me, but his concentration span is about twenty minutes. He wants me to be with him, but he doesn't have the concentration span to be in a deep place with anybody for very long. I know he loves and appreciates me, and I seem to be dependent on his presence in my life. This is horrible and maybe I'm being completely selfish, but if he could somehow be in my life the way he is and not involved with me every single day, I'd be a lot happier. I told him that his restlessness and distraction is pulling me into restlessness and distraction. I think this dream about Frank Sinatra hit on all this. I come from a family with a lot of turmoil and tragedy. My mother was so torn by depression and a bad marriage that she couldn't access deep concentration for very long. But my father and sisters had an extremely deep capacity for concentration. We were all very capable of focusing on each other; certainly, my grandparents were very focused on me. I think that's why Bob played such a huge role in my emotional life. Sinatra also reminds me of my first husband, who's gone from marriage to marriage. I think you [the therapist] have that capacity to go into depth and focus. You can be there and not get restless or have to move out of it because of discomfort with feelings. I think that Sinatra might be me, too, because I'm distracted by the outside world of friends and activities. I want my world to revolve around the deeply contemplative me and the real energy that comes out of that. I want to share those parts of myself with people in a genuine way that has some depth and meaning. I have to deal with the Frank Sinatra part of myself and go on to another life. My fantasy is to move to a place of my own where I can write and enter my deepest self. But I don't want to be all by myself—I still want my husband and friends in my life. Maybe I'm Sinatra's son because I'm drawing more heavily right now on my relationship with my father than with my mother. My father was in far better shape than my mother. He was highly functional and self-realized in a number of ways. I'm identifying with his vitality, humor, and creativity. I want to have his focus and depth of concentration. My book is about a state of meditative contemplation, and I think my happiness lies in having a deeply contemplative life with a male partner who can do the same.

The client began her associations referring to a former boyfriend, Bob, who played Frank Sinatra records. Bob had the capacity to focus attentively on her. Her book was about achieving a relationship with someone who could reach a deep level of mutual understanding and emotional rapport. However, her husband was distractible and could not focus on her in the way she desired. On the other hand, her father and sisters were able to interact with her on a deep level of emotional understanding. At this point, she referred to her therapist, whom she believed was able to focus on her with emotional depth and attentiveness. This was indicative of the positive transference she had with her therapist at the time. She returned to Sinatra and identified a part of herself with him, realizing that she, too, could be distractible and caught up in the activities of the outside world. Subsequently, she identified with her father's vitality, humor, and creativity. Toward the end of her associative stream, she wished for a greater depth of focus and concentration for herself, as well as for a mutually contemplative relationship with a male partner. This dream reflected elements of wish fulfillment, decision making, self-identity, transference, and relationships with others.

The following is an example of dream self-interpretation by a man who had previously been in therapy and worked with his dreams on a regular basis. He was a married professional and had the following dream shortly before his seventieth birthday:

> I was with a group of friends at a dinner party. We were engaged in lively conversation and having a good time. Suddenly, several strangers appeared among us and interrupted our party. Then, I noticed two men, both dressed in black, who seemed rather menacing. They came toward me, and I walked away from them. I was afraid they were going to harm me, and I started running. As they ran after me, I noticed my dog running beside me. I was hoping he would somehow protect me, when he suddenly changed into a German shepherd. He snarled at the two men and began to attack them. They ran away, and I felt very relieved.

The following are the dreamer's free associations and self-interpretation of the dream:

> This dream occurred on the night following a dinner party I attended with some close friends. One of my friends is exactly my age; in fact, we were born on the same day, month, and year. Both of us are approaching our seventieth birthdays, and we were discussing how it felt to be that age. Naturally, the conversation revolved around health issues, the recent deaths of mutual acquaintances, and how we wanted to live at this stage of life. I happened to notice that two of my friends were dressed in all black clothes—their jackets, shirts, and slacks were totally black. In fact, we even joked about it. One of them had open heart surgery not long ago. The other one has also had some recent health problems. I thought about my own health issues, especially an angioplasty I underwent a few months ago. Having had the heart procedure and approaching my seventieth birthday

has forced me to confront my mortality and to think about how I can make my remaining years as meaningful as possible. I think the menacing men in black represented death, my own future death. It's interesting how I transformed my dog, a mild-mannered Labrador retriever, into a snarling German shepherd. I guess it was a way to chase death away. Perhaps, I was calling on a part of myself to be aggressive and strong in my desire to live longer and to be as active and creative as I can be during the years I have left.

The dreamer began by associating to the dinner party with friends on the night of the dream. He noted that his seventieth birthday was approaching and that he shared it with one of his friends. Two of his friends were dressed in black at the party, and he and his friend with the same birthday discussed their recent health problems. The dreamer was reminded of his recent heart procedure and of his mortality. He thought that the men in black in his dream represented death, his own future death in particular. In transforming his dog into a snarling German shepherd who attacked the men in black, he felt that he was asking a part of himself to be aggressive and strong in his desire to live longer. He concluded that he wanted to be as active and creative as possible during his remaining years. This dream included self-representational, wish-fulfillment, relational, and decision-making elements.

COUNTERTRANSFERENCE DREAMS

At certain times during therapy, the therapist may be required to engage in self-interpretation when confronted with a countertransference dream. The latter may be extremely informative with regard to understanding the therapist's attitudes and feelings toward the client. Countertransference dreams can be especially helpful when the therapist is either experiencing projective identification or is involved in a countertransference enactment (Whitman, Kramer, and Baldridge 1969; Myers 1987; Gabbard 1995, 2004). In either instance, the therapist is responding cognitively, emotionally, or behaviorally to the internal state of the client. The communications or projections of the client induce the therapist to feel or act in an uncharacteristic manner. A countertransference dream usually portrays the client's internal conflict and emotional state, as well as the therapist's response to it.

The following is an example of self-interpretation and the use of a countertransference dream by a therapist:

A middle-aged man was in therapy for feelings of depression and low self-esteem. He believed that he was a failure in his career and interpersonal relationships. As a result, he was angry at himself and ashamed of not living up to his self-imposed standards. On the other hand, he was also critical and hostile toward others. This often took the form of caustic or demeaning comments to his wife, colleagues, and friends. His devaluation of others temporarily assuaged his low opinion of himself. Following a session with the client, his therapist dreamed the following:

> I found myself chasing Mike [the client] into a building. I knew he was in a rage, and he seemed intent on blowing up himself or the building. I tried to grab him and restrain him before he did it, but he was evasive, and I couldn't reach him. I felt helpless and frustrated.

The therapist's free associations and self-interpretation of the dream were as follows:

> I dreamt this the night following a session with Mike. The session centered mostly on his vicious criticism of his wife and a close friend. I was concerned that his wife might leave him because of his unrelenting criticism of her. We talked about past relationships that had ended because of his hostile behavior toward others. I think "blowing up" himself or the building in the dream is synonymous with his self-destructiveness and his tendency to wreck relationships. I told him during the session that he was like a "two-headed cobra" in that he could direct his lethal anger either toward himself or others. After I said that to him, I felt anxious because I thought the analogy was perhaps too extreme. I expected him to retaliate in some way, but he remained silent. Actually, he missed his next session, although he had a plausible excuse. Maybe he was acting out his anger at me. Sometimes, he can really make me uncomfortable, even annoyed with him, when he questions me excessively about something I've said or forgotten. He's an expert at making me feel stupid or wrong. Perhaps, the building is therapy, and I'm afraid he'll terminate or "blow up" the treatment. I do feel helpless and frustrated with him, as I did in the dream. I feel more anxious with him than angry. But maybe I'm afraid I'll explode with anger at him one of these days when he pushes my buttons. I think I'll let this dream percolate for awhile and, at the appropriate moment, tell him how the feelings he evokes in me are, perhaps, similar to his own.

The therapist's associations initially centered on the session preceding the dream. He was concerned about the client's vicious criticism of his wife and others. He felt that the imagery of blowing up himself and the building was analogous to the client's self-destructiveness, as well as his history of destroying other relationships. At this point, he recalled his observation to the client that he resembled a two-headed cobra. He wondered if this was too strong an analogy and the client might retaliate. Perhaps, the missed session was evidence of the client's acting out his anger at the therapist. His associations led to feelings that the client often evoked in him, namely feeling stupid or wrong. He acknowledged that he sometimes felt annoyed, frustrated, and helpless with the client, feelings similar to those he had in the dream. Then, the therapist wondered if the imagery of blowing up the building symbolized his fear that the client might terminate therapy. This led to his fantasy of exploding with anger at the client when he was provoked. Finally, the therapist decided to use his feelings about the client in a therapeutic way at an appropriate time.

The foregoing examples illustrate how free association and dream interpretation take place as a collaborative dialogue between client and therapist or as an inner dialogue within the dreamer. In each case, free association is the central process, whether or not facilitated by a therapist. This involves paying particular attention to the following elements in the dream: theme(s), activities, people, surroundings, feelings, behaviors, self, others, problems, issues, wishes, conflicts, and decisions. Past and present experiences are interwoven with each of these elements. The first two examples demonstrate the mutually collaborative process of free association, where the client and therapist engage in a dialogue revolving around these elements. The therapist focuses the client's attention on them by asking for elaboration, clarification, memories, and experiences in the past or present. In the first example, the therapist also inquired if the doctor in the dream displayed any of the qualities or characteristics of himself. This was a clear reference to the nature of the transference and led to the client's relationship with her uncle. The therapist eventually made a tentative interpretation toward the end of the associative dialogue, which the client accepted. In the second example, the therapist was more active in making interpretations during the session preceding the dream, as well as in the session devoted to the dream itself. In each example, the client used the therapist's interpretations to make further connections that were helpful. In the first instance, the client connected her feeling of being trapped and alone with her guilt over her sexual feelings and with her symptoms of depression and sleepiness. In the second example, the client made a connection between his feelings of abandonment and rejection and his symptoms of panic, anxiety, and insecurity.

The dreamers who self-interpreted engaged in a free-associative process or self-dialogue without the intervention of a therapist. Two of them were in therapy at the time of their dreams and reported their self-interpretations to the therapist. The first made a connection between a lack of love from his father and a supportive relationship with a former mentor that enabled him to develop the capacity for self-love and self-validation. The therapist speculated as to whether the client had also internalized beneficial qualities of the therapeutic relationship in the context of a positive transference. The second connected the theme of her novel about a search for mutual understanding and attentiveness to her husband's distractibility and lack of focus on her. She acknowledged her own difficulties with in-depth concentration and hoped to develop greater self-focus and autonomy, as well as a deeper relationship with a male partner. The third dreamer had the benefit of previous therapy and made the connection between his approaching seventieth birthday and his fear of death. The dream enabled him to connect with a part of himself that had a strong desire to live out the rest of his life creatively and meaningfully. The fourth dreamer was a therapist who dreamed about the destructive aspects of his client's personality following a session that evoked specific feelings in him. He acknowledged that the client sometimes made him feel stupid or wrong. Moreover, he realized that his feelings of frustration and helplessness in the dream were similar to what he felt consciously with the client. Finally, he recognized the potential of his own anger to erupt at the client, like the latter's rage at himself and others. The therapist decided to use his countertransference as characterized in the dream constructively at an appropriate time in the future with the client.

In summary, free association and interpretation are the essential components of constructive work with dreams either in or outside of therapy. They entail a collaborative dialogue between therapist and client or an internal dialogue within the dreamer. Although interpretation of the dream is a desirable goal, more important are the connections, insights, and new perspectives gained by the dreamer during the associative process. Optimally, dream imagery consists of a metaphorical narrative that gives meaning to the dreamer's current or past experiences, conflicts, feelings, relationships, and self-identity. Free association and interpretation unlock that meaning for the benefit of the dreamer, and open the door for the possibility of change.

The following points may be helpful with regard to free association and interpretation, either in a collaborative dialogue between therapist and client or in connection with the dreamer's self-dialogue:

1. Free-associate to each element in the manifest content of the dream, including theme(s), activities, surroundings, behaviors, feelings, self, others, problems, issues, wishes, conflicts, and decisions.
2. Attempt to make connections between the dream elements and current or past experiences, memories, feelings, relationships, and situations.
3. Search for similar qualities and characteristics between the dreamer and others in the dream imagery. The presence of the dreamer or a displacement figure may indicate a self-state dream.
4. If the dream occurs during therapy, look for evidence of transference in the imagery and associations. The therapist (or client) may appear as him- or herself or as someone else. If there is transference material, consider how it might apply to other significant relationships in the client's life.

5. If the dream belongs to the therapist, keep in mind the possibility of countertransference issues. Look for displacements of the client or therapist in the dream imagery. In particular, keep in mind recent sessions, feelings, and interactions with the client.

6. If therapy is at an impasse, and little or no movement is taking place, search for evidence of resistance in the dream imagery. The underlying reasons for the resistance may be discovered in its imagery or associations to it. One manifestation of resistance may be a reluctance or inability to free-associate to the dream.

7. Although interpretation is a desirable goal of the associative process, it is not the most important one. Of greater importance are the emotions, connections, different perspectives, and insights arrived at by means of the collaborative dialogue or the self-dialogue.

8. If the dream cannot be understood at the time it is recalled or reported, continue to have the client or dreamer free-associate to it. Sometimes, the associative process continues for days, weeks, or even months before a dream's full meaning becomes clear.

9. For purposes of validation in the case of self-interpretation, it is usually helpful to discuss the dream with a therapist if the dreamer is in active treatment. If he or she is not, the dreamer may wish to discuss it with a trusted friend.

REFERENCES

Bonime, W. 1986. Collaborative dream interpretation. *J. of the American Academy of Psychoanalysis* 14, no. 1:15–26.

Freud, S. 1911 [1958]. The handling of dream interpretation in psychoanalysis. In *The standard edition of the complete psychological works of Sigmund Freud*, ed. and trans. J. Strachey, Vol. 12, 91–96.

———. 1922 [1958]. Remarks on the theory and practice of dream interpretation. In *The standard edition of the complete psychological works of Sigmund Freud*, ed. and trans. J. Strachey, Vol. 19, 109–21.

Gabbard, G. O. 1995. Countertransference: The emerging common ground. *International J. of Psychoanalysis* 76:475–85.

———. 2004. Identifying and working with countertransference. In *Long-term psychodynamic psychotherapy*, 131–151. Washington, D.C. London: American Psychiatric Publishing.

Kantrowitz, J. L., A. L. Katz, and F. Paolitto. 1990. Follow-up of psychoanalysis five to ten years after termination: II. Development of the self-analytic function. *J. of the American Psychoanalytic Association* 38, no. 3:637–54.

Myers, W. A. 1987. Work on countertransference facilitated by self-analysis of the analyst's dreams. In *The interpretations of dreams in clinical work*, ed. A. Rothstein. Monograph 3, 37–46. Madison, CT: International Universities Press.

Natterson, J. M. 1980. The dream in group psychotherapy. In *The dream in clinical practice*, ed. J. M. Natterson, 435–43. New York: Jason Aronson.

Sloane, P. 1979. *Psychoanalytic understanding of the dream*. New York: Jason Aronson.

Ullman, M. 1987. The dream revisited: Some changed ideas based on a group approach. In *Dreams in new perspective: The royal road revisited*, ed. M. L. Glucksman and S. L. Warner. pp.119–30. New York: Human Sciences Press.

Viederman, M. 1991. The real person of the analyst and his role in the process of psychoanalytic cure. *J. of the American Psychoanalytic Association* 39, no. 2:451–89.

Whitman, R. M., M. Kramer, and B. J. Baldridge. 1969. Dreams about the patient: An approach to the problem of countertransference. *J. of the American Psychoanalytic Association* 17:702–27.

SUGGESTED READING

Bonime, W. 1989. *Collaborative psychoanalysis*. Cranbury, NJ: Associated University Presses.

Bonime, W., with F. Bonime. 1962[1982]. *The clinical use of dreams*. New York: Basic Books/DeCapo Press.

French, T. M., and E. Fromm. 1964. *Dream interpretation*. New York: Basic Books.

12

The Dream as a Facilitator of Change

DREAMS AND PSYCHOTHERAPY

The preceding chapters collectively emphasize the importance of the dream as a window into our interior mental life. Clinical and research data demonstrate that dreaming serves a variety of mental functions, including memory processing, learning, conflict resolution, problem solving, decision making, mood regulation, and psychological adaptation (Breger, Hunter, and Lane 1971; Palombo 1978; Cartwright 1986; Kramer 1993; Koulack 1993; Smith 1993; Hobson 1999; Reiser 2001). Collectively, these functions articulate with significant variables in psychotherapy (Luborsky et al. 1971; Kernberg et al. 1972; Bachrach, Weber, and Solomon 1985; Karasu 1986; Weiss 1993). For example, the major goal of psychotherapy is to enable the individual to resolve central conflicts and problems. In addition, psychotherapy is fundamentally a learning experience in which the client develops insight, effective coping strategies, mastery, and improved functioning. These, in turn, lead to greater self-esteem, more self-confidence, healthier interpersonal relationships, and improved adaptive capability. Psychotherapy also facilitates improved access to inner emotions, as well as more spontaneous, appropriate expressions of feelings. Moreover, during psychotherapy connections are made between present and past experiences that are vital to understanding irrational beliefs and behavior. In order to make these connections, the use of recent, past, explicit, and implicit memory are necessary. Dreaming involves similar components of memory, with frequent juxtapositions of recent and past events. During dreaming, explicit and implicit memory may be used for the purpose of conflict resolution and problem solving.

Although there are similarities between psychotherapy and dreaming, there are also significant differences. Psychotherapy requires that two or more participants engage in a verbal dialogue at the conscious level of experience (although unconscious material may emerge during the process). Dreaming is a uniquely personal activity, involving unconscious mentation during sleep. It occurs repetitively, on a nightly basis, governed by a biological substrate that is observed in all mammals. Psychotherapy, on the other hand, is not an intrinsic biological activity; it is a voluntary cognitive-emotional-behavioral process that requires interaction with others. The major goal of psychotherapy is change, including a reduction of symptoms, successful resolution of conflicts and problems, an improved sense of self, healthier interpersonal relationships, and more effective functioning. It is a learning experience that utilizes insight, cognitive reorganization, emotional regulation, and behavioral conditioning. Although dreaming appears to have certain functions in common with psychotherapy, change does not appear to be its primary purpose. However, dreams do seem to play an important role in learning, memory storage, problem solving, and mood stabilization. To the extent that dreaming involves these functions, dreaming has the potential to serve as a self-therapeutic experience. Of course, this occurs outside of conscious awareness and can only be integrated consciously if the dream is recalled and processed. Nevertheless, there is the possibility that dreaming facilitates change at an unconscious level, and experimental evidence suggests that this may be the case.

R. Greenberg et al. (1992, 1993) conducted a series of elegant experiments demonstrating that problems and conflicts encountered the preceding day were solved during that night's dreaming. R. D. Cartwright's (1991) research on divorcing couples indicates that those who dream more about their spouses while going through the divorce demonstrate improved function following the divorce compared to those who have fewer such dreams. M. Kramer's (1993) studies show that intense feelings, especially negative ones, are often neutralized during dreaming. If they are not successfully regulated, the person will likely awaken in a bad mood the next day. E. Hartmann (1996) examined repetitive dreams following an acute trauma (rape, fire, death of a comrade in combat) and observed that those occurring immediately after the trauma replay it as it was experienced. However, over the course of weeks and months, the emotions and events in the dreams change until the original trauma plays little or no role, and the feelings are transformed into more benign ones. This seems to be the pattern for the repetitive dreams associated with the successful resolution of posttraumatic stress disorder. The major functions of these repetitive dreams include replaying, neutralizing, and integrating the trauma in order for normal adaptive functioning to return.

The creative aspects of dreaming are reflected in the anecdotal reports of individuals, particularly artists and scientists, whose ideas and solutions to problems first appeared in their dreams (Garfield 1995). Some of the clinical examples in previous chapters demonstrate how problem solving and decision making may first take place in a dream prior to conscious awareness. Change, then, can be signaled, or at least facilitated, by dreams. However, systematic change with regard to symptoms, personality structure, self-concept, and relationships can only be brought about by psychotherapy. Nevertheless, dreams can be used as a powerful adjunct in the context of psychotherapy. They may confront the dreamer with major conflicts or dilemmas in a metaphorical, sometimes dramatic fashion. Inner feelings may be experienced either symbolically or directly, with intensity or subtlety. Qualities of the self and relationships with others may be portrayed honestly and accurately, sometimes exaggeratedly, as if to make a point. Issues, decisions, insights, and mental states may be depicted with great clarity. Dream imagery is replete with wishes, needs, sexual pleasures, fears, miraculous feats, and unimaginable horrors that remind us of our humanness and vulnerability. This material can be used by both therapist and client in psychotherapy to facilitate insight as well as to bring about change. It can also be employed outside of psychotherapy in order to monitor a dreamer's inner mental life for the purpose of enhancing self-awareness and promoting change. In other words, dreams provide a nightly menu of various facets of our psychological self-experience, which we are free to choose from in order to understand ourselves in greater depth and to help ourselves change.

MANIFEST IMAGERY

In some dreams, the manifest imagery is transparent and requires little, if any, free association. For example, in the dream in which a woman found herself swimming with her former husband on her back, the metaphorical message was that her husband's dependency and lack of cooperation in the marriage weighed heavily on her. She used this dream to confront him with his behavior and eventually divorced him when he failed to become more of an equal partner in the marriage. Another example of transparent imagery was the daughter who dreamed that she confronted her screaming mother and told her, "Tough, but I'm getting out anyhow." Her mother was extremely controlling and mentally disturbed. After years of catering to her needs, the daughter realized she had to emancipate herself from her subservient role in the relationship. The dream highlighted this issue, enabling her to change her behavior with her mother and to become more independent of her.

In other dreams, the manifest imagery is less transparent, but understanding its meaning requires minimal effort: for example, the unhappily married man involved with another woman who dreamed that he came to a fork in the road and had to choose which one to take. The dream confronted him with the emotional pain he was causing both women, as well as himself, by procrastinating in making a decision. The dream, which occurred while he was in therapy, spurred him to work through his feelings toward both women. As a result, he eventually divorced his wife and later married the other woman. Another example of thinly veiled manifest imagery was the dream of a busy physician who found himself in a rushing river trying to save others who were drowning. He was unable to do so and felt powerless to help. The dream forced him to realize how overworked he was in his practice and how socially isolated he had become because of his busy work schedule. Subsequent to the dream, he took steps to reduce his patient load and began to reach out to friends whom he had previously neglected. A further example of near transparent imagery was the dream of a woman in which a two-headed pig appeared. One head was that of a cute baby pig, while the other was that of a mean-looking wild boar. She realized that the pig represented two sides of herself: on the one hand, she could be sweet and kind, while on the other, she could be selfish and vicious. The self-confrontation presented by this dream began a prolonged self-exploration with the help of her therapist. Similarly, a young attorney in therapy dreamed that he was part of Hitler's entourage in a bloody battle with bayonets and hand-to-hand fighting. The imagery confronted him with his extreme competitiveness at work, which alienated him from his colleagues. Further associations to Hitler led him to explore his relationship with his father, who expected perfection and punished him when he failed to excel. As a result, he set high standards for himself and was fiercely competitive with others. This insight helped him to become less demanding of himself and less aggressive with his colleagues.

MANIFEST AND LATENT CONTENT

The imagery in most dreams is not as transparent as it is in these examples and requires the dreamer to free-associate more extensively; that is, to access the latent content. Take, for example, the older woman suffering from anxiety who dreamed that a tiger suddenly jumped out and terrified her. She was married for the second time following her first husband's death from a chronic, painful illness. She associated the tiger to her feeling of helplessness in the face of a potentially horrible death. Her second husband was older than she, and she realized that she was afraid that he, too, could die of a prolonged illness as her first husband had. Once she understood the meaning of the dream, she was able to reassure herself and reduce her anxiety with the knowledge that her current husband was in good health. Another example was the young man who kept sabotaging his career with indecision and procrastination. He dreamed that a plane taxied down the runway but couldn't take off. The plane represented a part of him that was paralyzed and ineffective with regard to his work. This insight helped him to explore his fear of failure and his use of procrastination to protect him from the humiliation connected to it.

Somewhat more complex was the imagery of a unicorn on a necklace in the dream of a nun who was struggling with her sexual feelings. She had entered a religious order subsequent to an attempted date rape in college. After a number of years in the religious community, she found herself tormented with guilt over her sexual fantasies. She associated the unicorn to virginity, purity, and her vows of chastity. On the other hand, she recalled that the unicorn also represented sexual potency. In the dream, she had wanted to buy the necklace, but decided not to. The dream focused her on the source of her guilt over sexual pleasure, namely her mother, who was puritanical and warned her of the dire consequences connected with sex. Her fear of punishment for her sexual desires was enacted in the attempted rape by her boyfriend in college. With the help of her therapist, she was able to work through her fears and inhibitions about experiencing sexual pleasure. Eventually, she was able to leave the religious community and began dating again. She engaged in sexual intercourse for the first time without feeling guilty, and ultimately married a man with whom she had developed a meaningful relationship. The unicorn imagery in the dream helped to focus her on her sexual conflict, facilitating an exploration of her feelings of guilt and fear connected to sexual pleasure.

DREAMS AND CLINICAL DIAGNOSIS

Certain dreams can be used to clarify a clinical diagnosis or to signal an impending crisis. For example, a professional man in his thirties developed atypical chest pain. A medical workup, including a cardiac evaluation, was normal. A psychiatric evaluation was inconclusive regarding a clinical diagnosis. During his initial interview, he reported the following dream: "I've killed somebody, but nobody knows I did it. I feel very guilty and am afraid of being found out." He had recently joined his father's professional firm with the understanding that he would eventually take it over. However, his father had a longtime associate, and he was concerned about the associate's feelings regarding his entering the firm. About six months prior to his joining the firm, the associate had a heart attack and died. In discussing the dream, he recalled that before joining the firm, he had consciously fantasized that if the associate died, it would make it easier for him to join his father. He became aware of how guilty he felt that the associate did die and that his fantasy was realized. He felt like a secret murderer and expected to be punished with a heart attack, like the associate. It became clear that his atypical chest pain was a conversion symptom, and he was diagnosed with a conversion disorder. The chest pain was a physical manifestation of his guilt and the retribution he expected. As a result of this insight and further therapy, he resolved his guilt, and his chest pain disappeared.

An older man complained of frequent memory lapses and repetitive nightmares that awakened him. On clinical examination, no definitive diagnosis could be made. He reported that in one of his dreams, he was planning a trip. However, he had difficulty finding the belongings he was to pack, then lost his way while driving. He awakened feeling confused, lost, and frustrated. The manifest imagery of this dream reflected his conscious experience of frequent memory lapses and confusion. An MRI and psychometric testing revealed that he had vascular dementia secondary to multiple, small infarcts in his brain. Once this diagnosis was made, the appropriate supportive treatment was initiated.

A middle-aged woman consulted her physician for feelings of fatigue. However, her sleep, appetite, and mood seemed normal. A medical workup was unremarkable. During her initial interview with a psychiatrist, she related the following dream: "I was walking up a hill carrying a suitcase. It felt heavy, and I could hardly move my feet." A mental-status examination revealed slowed cognition and impaired concentration. She admitted that she was indecisive and had lost interest in her usual activities. Furthermore, she had recently lost her job, and her dog had died. It became clear that she was suffering from an atypical major depression. The dream imagery metaphorically portrayed her impaired mental state and provided a clue to her underlying condition. Psychotherapy and antidepressant medication enabled her to recover from her depression.

Another woman had a history of a rapidly cycling bipolar disorder. In particular, her manic episodes seemed to occur precipitously, without warning. As a result, it was difficult to anticipate them and to adjust her mood-stabilizing medication accordingly. During one therapy session, she reported the following dream: "I was at a dance and saw a beautiful woman with long hair. She nodded at me, and I think she and I became the same person. A man asked me to dance, and we began whirling around. I felt like I was Cinderella." She recollected being told that she was the least attractive of her sisters, like Cinderella. During her manic episodes, she often developed a delusional belief that she was a glamorous actress. She felt elated and almost out of control in the dream. This alerted her psychiatrist to an impending manic episode, and he increased the dosage of her medication. As a consequence, she did not become manic, and her mood remained appropriate. In this instance, the dream imagery was a prologue to a developing manic state. It served as a warning signal for her psychiatrist, who, in turn, adjusted her medication and prevented a manic episode from occurring.

A woman was in treatment for recurrent depression, suicidal impulses, and self-mutilation. The latter consisted of frequent superficial cutting of her wrists and legs with a knife. She was physically and sexually abused by her father as a child but had forgotten most of those experiences. Her therapist was often uncertain as to when she was about to make a serious suicide attempt. She reported the following dream during one of her therapy sessions: "My legs were covered with cuts that had been sutured. I saw a little girl standing near me who was crying and covered in blood. I wanted to help her, but I couldn't move because my legs hurt so much. I was afraid she was going to die." She associated the little girl to herself and her childhood abuse. During much of her childhood and adult life, she experienced an inner emotional numbness. This appeared to be a depersonalized state that protected her from the intense fear and rage she felt toward her father. Cutting herself resulted in physical pain that, at least, enabled her to feel something in contrast to her pervasive inner emotional emptiness. It was also an enactment of her rage at her father and self-punishment for the guilt she felt over her sexual activity with him. She admitted to her therapist that she planned to cut her wrists so deeply that she would bleed to death. Moreover, she felt helpless and unable to stop herself from doing so (similar to her immobilization in the dream). With her consent, her therapist hospitalized her following this session. The dream signaled to both the client and her therapist that she was acutely suicidal. It also led to an understanding of the salient psychodynamic sources of her rage, guilt, self-mutilation, and depersonalization.

DREAMS, CORE CONFLICTS, AND PSYCHODYNAMICS

Core conflicts and psychodynamics are frequently revealed by manifest and latent dream content. Consider, for example, the young woman who dreamed that a Japanese woman attacked her while she was making love to her boyfriend. The dreamer had a history of failed romantic relationships and difficulties with female colleagues. She associated the Japanese woman to her mother, who was a painter and spent a good deal of time in Japan studying art. Her parents were divorced, and her mother was extremely bitter toward her father and men in general. As a consequence, the dreamer developed a distrust of men and was cynical about marriage. Moreover, she felt her mother was jealous of her relationship with her father and envious of her achievements. She believed that her mother would react with murderous rage toward her if she became more successful than she, professionally and romantically. Her awareness of this deep-seated belief helped her to understand why she sabotaged relationships with men and viewed other women as dangerous competitors. The dream served as a reference point for this central conflict and facilitated a change in her subsequent relationships with men and women.

An unmarried middle-aged man was in therapy because of an inability to commit himself in his relationships with women. He inevitably left each relationship because he ultimately found excessive faults with his partner. He was deliberating leaving his current girlfriend, Susan, when he dreamed the following: "I was lying in bed with Susan. We were in my parents' house where I grew up. The bedroom door was half open, and I could see another empty room across the hall. My father was standing by the door and said something objectionable. I was irritated with him and spoke to him harshly. Then, I became afraid that he would turn on Susan and me." He associated the empty room to his feelings of loneliness and fear of abandonment as a child. Both parents worked, and he spent a great deal of time at home alone. His father, an alcoholic, was often angry and frightening when he drank. His mother confided in him about her unhappiness with his father, and he slept in the same bed with her until he was twelve, while his father was out drinking. He recalled his conscious wishes as a boy to confront his father but was afraid of his father's anger. Moreover, he was terrified that his father would kill him if he found out that he slept with his mother and that she had confided in him about her dissatisfaction with the marriage. He realized that Susan was a displacement of his mother in the dream. Further associations led to his conviction that in each of his relationships, he unconsciously identified the woman with his mother in some way. As a result, committing to a relationship articulated with his childhood beliefs that he would either be abandoned by his family or killed by his father. His pattern of leaving relationships protected him from these potential catastrophes. The insight provided by this dream, as well as other clinical material, helped him to remain in the relationship with Susan (whom he eventually married).

The initial dreams of treatment often illuminate the underlying psychodynamics of the client's central conflict. For example, a married woman entered therapy with feelings of anxiety and inadequacy, especially at work and socially. She was obsessed with her physical appearance and worried that her husband might have an affair. She reported the following dream in her first therapy session: "I was at a concert where a woman conductor was leading an all-female chorus. My husband was in the audience, and I looked for his secretary in the chorus. Then, I realized that the conductor was me." The client's associations led to her interest in music and singing. She had an older sister, however, who was more talented musically and obtained better grades in school. Her father often commented that she had the "looks" in the family, but that her sister had the "brains" and musical ability. Throughout her childhood, and even as an adult, she competed with her sister for her father's attention and compliments. At work and in social situations, she always compared herself with other women in regard to her intelligence and attractiveness. She was particularly threatened by her husband's relationships with other women, especially his secretary. The image of herself as the conductor led to the realization that she had an excessive need to dominate and compete with other women, especially in the presence of men. This dream facilitated an understanding of the origins of her feelings of inadequacy, competitiveness with other women, and jealousy of her husband's relationships with them.

DREAMS AND FEELINGS

The imagery in the majority of dreams reflects feelings either directly or indirectly. An example of the direct experience of feeling was in the dream of a man the night before he was to give a presentation. He dreamed that he was about to be boiled alive by hostile cannibals. He was so terrified during the dream that he was awakened out of it. The stark terror he experienced in the dream reflected how fearful he was of the audience's potential criticism. His associations led to his fear of making a mistake in front of his highly critical, demeaning father. However, his subsequent experience with a benignly supportive male therapist enabled him to become less anxious when performing in front of others.

In other dreams, feelings may be expressed more symbolically. Consider, for example, the man who dreamed that while he was visiting a friend, someone stole his car and smashed it into another one. After confronting the thief, he returned to his friend, who had apparently left. The imagery of the man smashing his car into another one reminded him of his own temper, which often led to ruptured relationships. His friend's absence led him to recall his father's abandonment of him after his parents' divorce. He realized that the source of much of his anger revolved around the divorce and his feeling of being cheated out of a normal childhood (the stolen car). Moreover, his father was emotionally remote and unaffectionate. Following the dream, he had several therapy sessions with his father and expressed his feelings of betrayal, abandonment, and lack of paternal love. His father acknowledged that he had been unsupportive and had difficulty showing his love for his son. Subsequent to his confronting his father, their relationship improved, and his anger diminished. His relationships with others became less contentious and more cooperative.

Emotions are frequently both experienced and symbolized in the same dream. An example is the woman who found herself alone and terrified in the middle of the ocean with giant waves crashing over her. She tried to cling to some rocks, but her hands kept slipping off, and she was afraid she would drown. Her predominant feelings were terror and aloneness. At the time of the dream, she was so depressed that she was considering suicide. She associated the power and intensity of the giant waves to her suicidal impulses. They also represented the rage and self-punitive urges she felt, which were connected to guilt over past sexual promiscuity and several abortions. The dream helped her to focus on the rage and guilt that fueled her suicidal ideas. Over time, and with the aid of her therapist, she was able to feel less angry and guilty. As a result, her suicidal urges subsided.

Whether they are experienced or symbolized in manifest imagery, feelings are a reliable guide to the dreamer's internal emotional state. In the same way that they serve as an index to inner fear, rage, depression, or guilt, they can also alert the dreamer to a state of well-being. Consider the woman who was grieving for her dead brother and dreamed that she was walking through a field of flowers in Provence. She felt peaceful in the dream and associated Provence to a family vacation with her brother when she was happy. The dream informed her that she had resolved her grief over her brother's death and was feeling more optimistic about her life. Following this dream, she became more interested in her job and resumed her social activities. Another example was the young man who dreamed that he was snowboarding alone, feeling peaceful and happy. He was shy and socially anxious, particularly in school, where he was often teased. He was intimidated by an ill-tempered father and teased by his older brother. The dream occurred at a point in his therapy when he felt more self-confident and assertive. Snowboarding, a solitary activity that he excelled at, required little interaction with others. Nevertheless, as pleasant as the feelings in the dream were, it served as a reminder that he needed to work on feeling more secure and comfortable socially. A similar example of a dream that reflected the dreamer's inner emotional state, while at the same time serving as a reminder, was the woman dancing with a man on her left. They were gliding along smoothly, and she had a pleasant, loving feeling. The dreamer was unhappily married and was in treatment with a male therapist. At the time of the dream, she was having romantic fantasies about him. He was empathic and supportive, while her husband was critical and rejecting. However, she associated his dancing to her left as opposed to her right with the inappropriateness of pursuing her fantasies about developing an intimate relationship with him outside of therapy. Further exploration revealed that her father and other men had been abusive to her. Her relationship with the therapist was the first in which she had experienced a man as understanding and caring. The dream enabled her to realize that a relationship with a man could be different. Ultimately, she divorced her husband with the knowledge that there was the possibility of a healthier relationship with another man.

DREAMS, RELATIONSHIPS, AND SELF

Although the imagery in the previous examples included themes of the self and relationships with others, certain dreams are more dramatic and specific than others in highlighting these elements. They can be particularly helpful in focusing the dreamer on aspects of self in the context of relationships. Sometimes, the dreamer or others appear as themselves; at other times, there is a displacement onto another person, animal, or object. More rarely, the dream is exclusively about the self (self-state dreams). An example of the latter was the two-headed pig representing the dreamer's sweet, tender qualities, as well as her greedy, vicious ones. The power of this imagery forced the dreamer to confront those qualities in herself that she preferred to deny. Another was the man who dreamed he was going to have surgery for a brain tumor. He felt numb and stuporous in the dream. The surgery represented the therapy he was beginning for difficulty in experiencing and expressing his feelings. Indeed, the numbness and stupor he felt in the dream accurately reflected his inner sense of emotional emptiness. In both of these examples, the dreamer and therapist often referred to these self-portrayals during the course of treatment.

   More often than not, dream imagery reflects oneself interacting with others. An example was the man who dreamed he was riding a bike with a friend who fell off his. He felt superior and gloated over his friend's misfortune. The dreamer actually felt inferior to many of his friends and colleagues. However, he protected himself by behaving in a superior, condescending fashion with them. The dream helped him to trace the development of these traits to his relationship with his father. The latter often humiliated him for his mistakes and physical awkwardness. A great deal of time in his therapy was devoted to changing his expectation of criticism and humiliation from others. Another example was the chronically ill woman who dreamed that her husband and doctors were at her bedside but seemed oblivious to her condition and offered no help. In fact, she felt that her husband was insensitive to her needs and that her doctors were indifferent to her suffering. Further exploration revealed that her parents were inattentive and unloving during her childhood. As an adult, she expected others to behave the same way toward her. Over the course of treatment, she gradually came to believe that her therapist genuinely cared about her. She was subsequently able to extend this belief to her husband and doctors.

Dream imagery that portrays the interaction between oneself and others provides an opportunity for the dreamer to examine specific qualities of self and how they influence relationships. Consider the man who dreamed that while playing golf, he swung at a ball and missed. He was so embarrassed that he stopped playing and walked away from his golfing partners. He was a perfectionist and abhorred any kind of mistake or failure in himself or others. As a result, friends and colleagues found him competitive and judgmental. Further associations to the dream led to his relationship with his father, who was harsh and punitive. As a child, he tried to do everything perfectly in order to avoid his father's criticism and punishment. The dream served as a catalyst for him to reassess his excessive expectations of himself and others. Therapy enabled him to diminish the influence of the internal judgmental image of his father so that he became less demanding of himself and those around him. A similar example was the woman who dreamed that she was hiking with her sister when a gigantic, horned snake lunged out and bit her. The dream occurred shortly after her roommate had had a prolonged telephone conversation with her boyfriend, arousing her jealousy. She identified her roommate with her younger sister, whom her father began to favor when the dreamer reached adolescence. Being bitten by the snake represented the betrayal and pain she felt when her father shifted his attention to her sister. From then on, she tended to feel jealous and distrustful of her girlfriends. This insight helped her to realize that neither her roommate nor her other friends were trying to steal the affection of her boyfriend. As a consequence, she became more trusting and friendly toward them.

Other dreams may validate the dreamer's self-image and interactions with others. Consider the professor who was being considered for tenure and dreamed that his chairman told him he was going to receive an academic award. He felt pleased and recognized for his achievements in the dream. Actually, he was doubtful that he would receive tenure and was unsure of his chairman's evaluation of him. Although this was a wish-fulfillment dream, it encouraged him to feel more self-confident and hopeful. It also helped him to focus on his need to believe in his own capabilities. Similarly, the female musician who was insecure about her ability and career dreamed that she was in a piano-playing contest and won over another contestant. When she asked a respected colleague why she had won, he replied, "Because you're the best." This was also a wish-fulfillment dream that helped to affirm the dreamer's belief in her talent. Her parents neither supported nor encouraged her decision to become a musician, eroding her self-confidence. As a result, she depended on the impressions of her colleagues and teachers. The dream emphasized how important it was for her to develop an inner belief in her self-competence and musical abilities. A similar theme occurred in the self-interpreted dream of the physician who found himself in the medical school where he once taught. He thought he had witnessed some sort of illegal activity and sought out his chairman, Sam. While they walked arm in arm, he told him about the crime he had observed. His associations led him to recall the lack of love he felt from his father. Moreover, other teachers and mentors had disappointed him during his career. However, Sam was a supportive authority figure and treated him with kindness and respect. In that regard, he was the good father whom the physician had never had. He interpreted the criminal activity as symbolic of the mistreatment he had experienced with his father and his former mentors. As he worked with the dream, he realized that it was his responsibility to build on the positive feelings he had received from Sam and to use them in order to provide a self-generated inner love for himself.

DREAMS, DECISION MAKING, AND PROBLEM SOLVING

Decision-making and problem-solving dreams invariably contain imagery of the self, others, and feelings. However, their major theme involves a decision or solution on the part of the dreamer. Perhaps, more so than other dreams, they offer the dreamer an opportunity to take action and to effect change either internally or externally. Nevertheless, they should be understood primarily as metaphorical narratives that offer options to the dreamer rather than literal solutions. Whether or not the decisions and solutions in the dream are appropriate, they may provide the dreamer with information to explore the salient issues further and hopefully learn from that endeavor. Usually, by the time a problem-solving or decision-making dream occurs, the dreamer has already processed the issue for some time, consciously or unconsciously. This was the case with the divorced woman who dreamed that she was on a bus going from California to the East. The other passengers were fellow employees who were leaving her company because of downsizing. She decided to get off the bus because it was going in the wrong direction for her. In reality, she wanted to remain employed because she had to support herself and her son. In addition, she was in a relationship with a married man who refused to leave his wife. Although she lived in an Eastern city, she had fond memories of California where she had lived following her divorce, a period in her life when she felt free and independent. At the time of the dream, she had been deliberating the pros and cons of leaving her company and ending her relationship.

However, she felt the dream was telling her to remain with the company and to break off her relationship. Shortly after, she spoke with her supervisor, who helped her to find a more secure job within the company. Simultaneously, she ended her relationship with the married man. Although she might have reached the same decisions without the dream, it facilitated her taking action to make the necessary changes in her life. Another example was the woman unhappily married to an abusive husband. He refused to participate in marital therapy and would not acknowledge his destructive behavior. She dreamed that she was going on a trip with him, and a cab came to pick them up. She asked him if he would bring their luggage to the cab, but he told her to get it herself. She became angry and refused to go on the trip with him. She asked him to leave and put their children in bed with her. From her perspective, the imagery was a reflection of their marriage. She found herself continuously angry with him because of his lack of sensitivity and cooperation. Further associations reminded her of leaving home because of her verbally abusive father. Although she had considered divorce prior to the dream, it galvanized her to ask her husband for a separation. It also shored up her courage to seek custody of their children, even though he threatened to fight her for them.

Some decision-making dreams focus the dreamer on the necessity to make changes, even though the solution in the dream is unrealistic. Consider the female teacher who felt that the teaching methods used in her school were outmoded. She dreamed that a little boy knocked on her classroom door and asked to be let in. He said his name was "Opportunity." She took him to her principal and explained that she had no room in her class for him. However, the principal seemed uninterested and did not offer to help. The dreamer was new to her job and reluctant to make suggestions about more effective methods of teaching. While growing up, her parents referred to her as ugly and stupid. As a result, she developed a poor self-image and felt inhibited about expressing her opinions, especially to anyone in authority. She associated the little boy to herself because she had never felt pretty or feminine. Nevertheless, she believed she was telling herself to take the opportunity to offer suggestions to her principal about using different approaches to teaching. After some hesitation, she made an appointment with her principal and gave her opinions about the school's teaching agenda. To her surprise, the principal was open to her suggestions and expressed her appreciation. This experience provided a major boost to her self-confidence and enabled her to become more assertive. A similar example was the mother who felt that her relationship with her daughter was deteriorating because her job required her to spend a great deal of time away from home. She dreamed that she was driving over a bridge with her daughter when it began to sway. There were gaping holes in the road necessitating her to swerve the car in order to avoid them. Nevertheless, she decided to continue to drive over the bridge until she reached the other side. She associated the swaying bridge and potholed road to her problematic relationship with her daughter. Until the time of the dream, she had avoided discussing her feelings about their relationship with her daughter. Her major fear was that her daughter would express how angry she was over her long hours away from home, instead of spending more time with her. She had grown up in a family where differences of opinion and confrontation were avoided. Angry feelings, in particular, were strongly discouraged by her parents. The dream encouraged her to start a dialogue with her daughter concerning her guilt over neglecting her. Although her daughter expressed anger and disappointment with her, she also was grateful that her mother acknowledged an awareness of the problem. As a result of their conversation, the mother resolved to find ways to spend more quality time with her daughter. Another example was the woman who was an executive with a large corporation that was downsizing. She dreamed that a forest fire was approaching her house. Fearful that her house would catch on fire, she decided to run into the cellar and hide. She associated the fire to the imminent possibility that she could lose her job. Her usual way of dealing with stressful situations was to avoid or deny them. However, after reflecting on her behavior in the dream, she decided to confront her boss directly about her future. He responded candidly and told her that although her job would be eventually terminated, she could still count on another year of employment. Armed with this reassurance, her anxiety diminished, and she began a methodical job search.

Certain decision-making dreams confirm what the dreamer has already consciously decided but has not yet acted on. Or they may inform the dreamer of a decision that has already been preconsciously formulated. An example was the dream of a divorced woman who was in a relationship with a man but was ambivalent about ever remarrying. She dreamed that she was on a walking tour of Chicago where everything seemed very real. She found herself looking forward to seeing different buildings, streets, and familiar places. Throughout the dream, she had a good feeling. Her ambivalence about remarrying was connected to being rejected by her first husband, who left her for another woman. They had met in Chicago, where both attended college. Chicago connoted feelings of betrayal, rejection, and distrust of men. In the dream, however, she looked forward to her walking tour of the city where everything seemed very real, and she had a good feeling. She associated her changed outlook to the genuine love and trust she felt toward her present boyfriend. The dream solidified her conviction that this was a safer, more loving relationship than her first marriage. Shortly after the dream, she accepted her boyfriend's proposal of marriage. Another example was the widower who was reluctant to begin seeing other women several years after his wife's death. Although he had worked through his grief, he was doubtful that he could ever love another woman. He dreamed that he saw his children driving cars down impossible chutelike roads. They told him, "C'mon, pop, take more chances." He associated the chutelike roads to an amusement park ride his parents took him on as a child. His father told him he would be a brave boy if he went on the ride. His children had been encouraging him to meet other women, but he was hesitant to do so. He felt that he was telling himself to take the chance of starting a relationship with another woman. Despite his fears of another possible loss, he called a woman he had recently met and asked her to go out with him.

Certain dreams inform the dreamer of an internal mental state reached following a significant event, illness, or therapy. Consider the woman who became seriously depressed after her husband divorced her and dreamed that she went on a cruise with a friend. They were dressed in yellow pajamas, and she told her friend, "We're going to have fun." For her, the color yellow was connected to happiness and optimism. She and her friend had been discussing the possibility of taking a trip together when she felt better. The dream informed her that she was no longer depressed and that she could carry on an independent life without her former husband. A similar example was the dream of a young woman who was tortured with guilt after her alcoholic mother died in a fire. She felt she could have saved her mother if she had stayed home with her. In her dream, she was at a lake that she wanted to swim across. Her family doctor offered her a pair of flippers to use, but she declined and told him she could swim across the lake on her own. She had vacationed at the lake with her parents prior to their divorce. It was a happier time for her family, before her mother began drinking and her father had left. In addition to her guilt, she was angry at her father for abandoning them. She associated the doctor to her therapist, who had helped her to resolve her guilt and anger. Swimming across the lake on her own meant that she was ready to terminate therapy and no longer needed her therapist's support. The dream informed her that she had accepted her mother's death and reconciled with her father. Another example was the woman who dreamed that she was in a rowboat with her mother. She was struck by how charming and beautiful her mother was. Intense feelings of love and happiness enveloped her. The dreamer had suffered a series of losses from childhood, including her mother's repeated hospitalizations for mental illness. Her happiest memories were those of playing with her mother before she became mentally ill. As a writer, she struggled for many years to recapture the imaginative creativity and spontaneity she experienced as a child with her mother. Much of her therapy was focused on reconciling herself to her losses, especially the loss of her mother. At the time of the dream, she felt that she had internalized her mother's imagination, playfulness, and spontaneity. These qualities were reflected in a novel that she had just completed.

POSTTRAUMATIC DREAMS

The frequency and intensity of dreams following a physical or psychological trauma are reliable indicators of whether or not the dreamer has recovered from it. There is some controversy as to whether their diminished intensity and frequency reflects the reduction in dysphoric feelings connected to the trauma or whether the dreams themselves regulate these feelings. Regardless of the mechanisms involved, posttraumatic dreams correlate with clinical improvement, or the lack thereof, following a trauma. For example, consider the woman who swallowed glass in her salad and had repetitive dreams about broken glass in her mouth from the smashed windshield of a bus. As she improved and began frequenting restaurants again, the dreams gradually subsided. On the other hand, the woman who was sexually abused by her father and uncle continued to have frightening recurrent dreams of being held down by two men. These were correlated with symptoms of recurrent depression and depersonalization that failed to subside, despite treatment.

TRANSFERENCE DREAMS

Transference dreams are among the most meaningful and reliable indicators of change during psychotherapy. They portray the client's perceptions and feelings toward the therapist at any given time during treatment. Previous examples of early and later transference dreams include the one where the client initially viewed the therapist as an "evil force," then later as a man who helped her repair a bridge that was falling apart. Another example was a client's early dream in which the therapist had begun a session with another person, then a later dream where a professor was patient and understanding. The manifest imagery in each of these dreams reflected the changed perceptions of the client toward the therapist. Somewhat less transparent was a transference dream early in therapy of a man who was extremely competitive and distrustful of other men. He dreamed, "I was with a group of men in a hostile environment. We needed to cross a body of water in a country that was a dictatorship. An older man offered us his boat, but wanted us to pay $75 for it. We got into the boat and headed out to sea but didn't know what to do next." He associated the hostile environment and dictatorship to his family and his tyrannical, abusive father. The older man who asked for $75 was his

therapist, whom he did not initially trust and to whom he paid a fee. Moreover, he was afraid that his therapist might be critical and would reject him,
like his father. Heading out to sea and not knowing what to do next portrayed
his attitude toward therapy; it was uncertain, and he was a novice as a client.
A later transference dream followed: "I was traveling in Europe with you,
and everything was going well. I had a peaceful feeling." This dream occurred after his therapist had returned from a vacation in Europe. While the
therapist was away, he had fantasies of traveling with him as a son might
with a benevolent, loving father. At this point in treatment, he was more
trusting of his therapist and viewed him as an ally. Therapy had enabled him
to differentiate his therapist from his father; moreover, his actual experience
with the therapist as a noncritical, empathic person facilitated his trust. At
the same time, he felt less threatened by other men and was less competitive
toward them.

TURNING-POINT AND TERMINATION DREAMS

Turning point and termination dreams are, perhaps, the most dramatic and
significant dreams that occur during therapy. They represent the vanguard of
unconscious announcements concerning the most important decisions, insights, and changes in the client's personality and life. For example, consider
the woman who dreamed that she was on a bus going in the wrong direction
and got off. The dream informed her that she needed to keep her job and terminate an unsatisfactory relationship. This was a turning-point dream that facilitated her taking action based on her interpretation of the dream. Another
example was the nun who dreamed that she saw a statue of a unicorn and
found herself swimming freely in the ocean. This imagery and her associations to it confronted her with her conflicted feelings about her sexuality and
her wish to leave her religious community. This was also a turning-point
dream that enabled her to acknowledge her heterosexual desires and to begin
living a secular life. Certain turning-point dreams indicate a significant
change in the dreamer's internal emotional state; consider, for example, the
woman who was clinically depressed after her divorce and who dreamed
while on a cruise wearing yellow pajamas that she told her friend, "We're going to have fun." The color yellow and her happy, optimistic feelings in the
dream indicated that she was no longer depressed. Some turning-point
dreams reflect a significant change in the dreamer's pathological behavior,
such as that of the man who had been engaging in self-sabotaging behavior,
then dreamed that a plane taxied down the runway and was able to lift off.
This dream contrasted with a previous dream in which the plane was unable
to take off, reflecting his procrastination and indecisiveness. At the time of the

dream, he was no longer involved in self-sabotaging behavior. Change in self-identity may also be reflected in turning-point dreams. For example, a man came to therapy for anxiety and obsessive-compulsive behavior linked to fear of his mother's disapproval and rejection. His sense of self was dependent on pleasing others and gaining their approval. After several years of therapy, he dreamed, "I have a younger male therapist. I'm sad that you're not my therapist, but I don't feel resentful or panicked. I know that I'll be alright." The dream occurred shortly after a confrontation with his mother during which he told her that he was essentially being reparented by his therapist because of the hurt and damage she caused. He identified with the younger male therapist in the dream in that he felt competent enough to continue changing by means of a self-dialogue. At this point in treatment, he was no longer afraid of disapproval from his mother or others. He felt more confident and self-reliant, without the need for reassurance from external sources. This was both a transference and turning-point dream that portrayed his internalization of the healing aspects of the therapeutic relationship.

Termination dreams usually reflect a successful working through of central conflicts and demonstrate that the client can function independently of the therapist. For example, consider the woman who dreamed that she wanted to swim across a lake and refused the use of flippers offered her by her family doctor. Her associations led to her belief that she had resolved her guilt over her mother's death and was no longer angry at her father. Moreover, she felt that she was able to function without the help of her psychiatrist (the family doctor). Another example was the woman who dreamed that she was helped to board a plane safely by a man, even though a little girl had jumped to her death. She was traumatized in her childhood by a violent father and an emotionally distant mother. The little girl represented her own suicidal urges prior to treatment, and the man who helped her to safety was her therapist. At this point in therapy, she was no longer self-destructive and was more trusting in her relationships with others. Turning-point and termination dreams are among the most reliable tools available for the documentation of change during psychotherapy.

Although the previously outlined categories of dreams may seem somewhat arbitrary, they are based on clinical, pragmatic, and research considerations for the purpose of developing a methodology toward understanding and utilizing dreams in order to effect change. Regardless of whether dreams are explored within or outside of therapy, they can be utilized as powerful facilitators of change. They provide the dreamer with the opportunity to dwell temporarily within the deepest reaches of the unconscious. The metaphorical imagery experienced in the course of dreaming can be poetic, dramatic, incisive, and creative. The dreamer is immersed in conflicts, problems, emotions, self-identity issues, and relationships with others poignantly and honestly. More often than not, dream imagery can be bizarre, perplexing, and obscure. However, if the associative dialogue described in this book is methodically used by the client and therapist, or by the dreamer alone, the meaning of manifest and latent imagery has, at least, the potential to be understood. Naturally, many dreams cannot be deciphered and, perhaps, have no psychodynamic meaning at all. Some are too puzzling or confusing; others are simply replays of the preceding day's events. However, even those events or experiences chosen for replay, inconsequential as they seem, may have significance on closer examination. Although the desired goal of free association is an interpretive understanding of the dream, it is only one among the many benefits derived from working with manifest dream content. Of equal or greater importance are the different perspectives, connections, and insights gained from free-associating to current and past experiences, feelings, perceptions of self, and relationships. In turn, this process has the potential to expand the dreamer's self-awareness and, by doing so, constitutes change.

The assignment of meaning to conscious experience is a uniquely human activity. Understanding the meaning of unconscious experience affords us an even greater awareness of our humanness. Dreams provide us with that opportunity. Once we understand the meaning of a dream, we are afforded the possibility of translating it into internal, as well as external, change. Internal change affects our feelings, thoughts, perceptions, and beliefs. External change involves our behavior, interaction with others, and implementation of our decisions. Dreams provide us with a unique source of information in order to facilitate both internal and external changes. Sigmund Freud (1900) described the dream as "that most marvelous and most mysterious of all instruments" that illuminates the "royal road to a knowledge of the unconscious activities of the mind." If we follow that road, there are limitless possibilities to the ways in which we can understand and change ourselves. The goal of this book has been to acquaint therapists, clients, and others with the fascinating world of dreams, as well as with a methodology for deciphering and applying them in order to achieve greater self-knowledge and the capacity for change. The key to changing ourselves, and as a consequence the world in which we live, is contained within our dreams. They are always available to us and require only our curiosity and motivation to unravel their meaning and to use that information for our benefit.

REFERENCES

Bachrach, H., J. Weber, and M. Solomon, 1985. Factors associated with the outcome of psychoanalysis (clinical and methodological considerations) of the Columbia

Psychoanalytic Center research project (IV). *International Review of Psychoanalysis* 43:161–74.

Breger, L., I. Hunter, and R. Lane. 1971. *The effect of stress on dreams*. Psychological Issues 3. Monograph 27, 1–213. New York: International Universities Press.

Cartwright, R. D. 1986. Affect and dreamwork from an information processing point of view. *J. of Mind and Behavior* 7:411–28.

———. 1991. Dreams that work: The relation of dream incorporation to adaptation to stressful events. *Dreaming* 1:3–10.

Freud, S. 1900 [1958]. The interpretation of dreams. In *The standard edition of the complete psychological works of Sigmund Freud*, ed. and trans. J. Strackey Vol. 5, 608. London: Hogarth Press.

Garfield, P. 1995. *Creative dreaming*. New York: Simon and Schuster.

Greenberg, R., H. Katz, W. Schwartz, and C. Pearlman. 1992. A research-based reconsideration of psychoanalytic dream theory. *J. of the American Psychoanalytic Association* 40:531–50.

Greenberg, R., and C. Pearlman. 1993. An integrated approach to dream theory: Contributions from sleep research and clinical practice. In *The functions of dreaming*, ed. A. Moffitt, M. Kramer, and R. Hoffmann, 363–80. Albany: State University of New York Press.

Hartmann, E. 1996. Outline for a theory on the nature and functions of dreaming. *Dreaming* 6, no. 2:147–70.

Hobson, J. A. 1999. The new neuropsychology of sleep: Implications for psychoanalysis. *Neuro-Psychoanalysis* 1, no. 2:157–83.

Karasu, T. B. 1986. The specificity versus non-specificity dilemma: Toward identifying therapeutic change agents. *American J. of Psychiatry* 143, no. 6:687–95.

Kernberg, O., L. Coyne, L. Horwitz, A. Appelbaum, and E. Burstein. 1972. Psychotherapy and psychoanalysis: Final report of the Menninger Foundation psychotherapy research project. *Bulletin of the Menninger Clinic* 36:3–275.

Koulack, D. 1993. Dreams and adaptation to contemporary stress. In *The functions of dreaming*, ed. A. Moffitt, M. Kramer, and R. Hoffmann, 321–40. Albany: State University of New York Press.

Kramer, M. 1993. The selective mood regulatory function of dreaming: An update and revision. In *The functions of dreaming*, ed. A. Moffitt, M. Kramer, and R. Hoffmann, 139–95. Albany: State University of New York Press.

Luborsky, L., M. Chandler, A. Auerbach, J. Cohen, and H. M. Bachrach. 1971. Factors influencing the outcome of psychotherapy. *Psychological Bulletin* 75, no. 3:145–85.

Meissner, W. W. 1991. *What is effective in psychoanalytic therapy*. Northvale, NJ: Jason Aronson.

Palombo, S. R. 1978. *Dreaming and memory*. New York: Basic Books.

Reiser, M. 2001. The dream in contemporary psychiatry. *American J. of Psychiatry* 158:351–59.

Smith, C. 1993. REM sleep and learning: Some recent findings. In *The functions of dreaming*, ed. A. Moffitt, M. Kramer, and R. Hoffmann, 341–62. Albany: State University of New York Press.

Weiss, J. 1993. *How psychotherapy works*. New York: Guilford Press.

Index

abandonment, 36–37; anxiety stemming from, 67–68, 118–119; compulsive buying and, 121–122; in dreams, 37, 48–49, 92, 95, 105, 106, 119–126, 140–141, 144, 145–146. *See also* insecurity; isolation; rejection; vulnerability

activities in dreams, 15–16

adaptive function of dreaming, 58, 84

affect, 23

affection in dreams, 41–42, 88, 93–94, 99

affective attunement, 24

affirmation in dreams, 40–41, 60, 99–100, 105, 107, 124, 125, 126, 148–149. *See also* affection; confidence; success; well-being

aggression in dreams, 77, 79–80, 103, 104, 129–130, 140. *See also* anger; competition; conflict; injury

alexithymia, 28

ambivalence in dreams, 31, 105, 106. *See also* conflict

anger in dreams, 13, 26, 30, 62, 80, 85, 98–99, 131–132. *See also* aggression; competition; injury

anniversary dreams, 87–89; interpretation guidelines, 89–90

anxiety: panic attacks, 118–123; physiology, 67; problems stemming from, 68, 121–122; sources, 67–68, 118–119, 120–121. *See also* anxiety in dreams; trauma

anxiety in dreams, 26, 27, 30–31, 67–76, 103, 145; defense mechanisms and, 69, 120–121; interpretation guidelines, 75; physical sensations, 69–70; posttraumatic stress disorder dreams, 70–71, 86–87, 138, 143, 153; rejection as cause, 67–68, 72, 94, 121; stressful issues, 72–74. *See also* failure; insecurity; vulnerability

behavior in dreams, 15–16, 60, 61; derivative behavior in dreams, 77–78; self-identity dreams, 50–51, 74, 77–78; bizarre dreams, 54, 62

body image, 49–50

censorship mechanism, dreams as, 2, 6–7, 68–69, 77. *See also* latent content

change, 1; dreams and, 137–139; psychotherapy and, viii–ix, 137–157; resistance to, 96–97, 105, 106,

About the Author

Myron L. Glucksman, M.D. is a board-certified psychiatrist and psychoanalyst with more than forty years of clinical experience. He is a Training and Supervising Psychoanalyst at The Psychoanalytic Institute of New York Medical College where he is also a clinical professor of psychiatry. A past-president of The American Academy of Psychoanalysis and Dynamic Psychiatry, he maintains a private practice in Redding, Connecticut and New York City. Dr. Glucksman is coeditor of *Dreams in New Perspective: The Royal Road Revisited* (1987). He is actively engaged in clinical dream research, with a particular focus on how dreams can be used to access and facilitate clinical change during psychotherapy and psychoanalysis.